WILLIAM P. LYONS MASTER'S ESSAY AWARD

The William P. Lyons Master's Essay Award was established

in 1960 by the Department of History

of Loyola University, Chicago,

and the Loyola University Press.

The Award is made annually

to encourage significant work at the Master's level

in history in American universities.

It recognizes scholarship

that is exemplary in style and method,

based solidly on original sources

and interpretatively significant in current research.

HERBERT ALAN JOHNSON

The Law Merchant and Negotiable Instruments in Colonial New York 1664 to 1730

LOYOLA UNIVERSITY PRESS

Chicago, Illinois

1963

© 1963 Loyola University Press
Printed in the United States of America
Library of Congress Catalog Card Number: 62-20985

PREFACE

This brief study of the law merchant and bills of exchange in colonial New York has as its background a fascinating era of legal history. Changing legal institutions as well as newly developed methods and patterns of trade were typical of these early years. For the student of history, as well as the legal scholar, these developments are of great significance for they are the basis for future growth of the law and the commercial supremacy of the province of New York.

In the preparation of this study I am indebted to Professor Richard B. Morris for his invaluable guidance and assistance in directing my research. I have profited from the suggestions of

Professor Paul M. Hamlin of New York Law School and Professor Lawrence H. Leder of Brandeis University. Without the co-operation of the staffs at the New-York Historical Society, the New York Public Library, the Office of the City Clerk of New York City, and the Division of Records, New York County Clerk's Office, this study could never have been undertaken.

HERBERT A. JOHNSON

Columbia University

CONTENTS

INTRODUCTION

The law merchant, unlike many areas of jurisprudence, rarely develops in the austere environs of law office or judicial chamber. Far more colorful and informal are the backgrounds against which its story must be told. The quarterdeck of the brigantine splattered with the salty brine of the Atlantic, the frenzied activity in a quayside market, and the crisp methodical efficiency of a merchant's countinghouse are representative of the settings in which the historical novelist would set the action.

While this essay treats the changes in the law merchant and in negotiable instruments in early colonial New York, it must not be considered merely a study of local legal history. Rather it must be viewed in the broader context of the British Empire, in which New York was destined to play an ever-increasing role. Because of the formative influence of trade practice on mercantile law, it is essential that this study give due consideration to New York's commercial place in the empire of Great Britain.

Prosperity was not the lot of the province of New York in the years from 1664 to 1730, and we may be sure that at times her poorer inhabitants suffered the hardships that attend economic instability and depression. A critical lack of circulating currency plagued the early years, only to be succeeded by the inflationary issue of paper bills of credit. Throughout the period poor harvests and decreasing markets threatened the business economy of New York. Before Wall Street ceased to be a lane and became the scapegoat for all of the failings of the economy, there was felt in New York the impact of an empire-wide depression that followed in the wake of the financial manipulations of the South Seas Company. So tragic were the effects in the province that the "hard money" men in the General Assembly enacted provisions for the relief of the debtor class.

Financial cycles and unpredictable business conditions produce men of caution who extend credit only upon the most certain of security. It is not surprising that New York merchants clung to the old Dutch practice by securing loans through the formal writing obligatory. To be sure, they made the performance of the conditions of the loan even more imperative through the use of a penal provision providing for a forfeiture for nonpayment on the due date. In this state of the economy only small amounts were secured by the unceremonious promissory note, which had been recently introduced from England.

Predominantly coastal in its trade, New York had little opportunity to absorb the commercial practice or the law merchant of England. As a result the early bills of exchange were of the simplest form and the complex Dutch bill of exchange, used in the Amsterdam trade before the conquest, fell into disuse. Neither bills of exchange nor promissory notes seem to have been assigned during this period, a phenomenon due more to the lack of funds for rediscounting than to the legal rules concerning negotiability.

Economic influences and legal theory combined to form the New York law of negotiable instruments during the colonial period. That the legal theory was an amalgam of Dutch civil law and elementary English common law serves to complicate the situation. Furthermore, the unsettled nature of the judicial system during the seventeenth century made consistent legal development fortuitous at its best, and haphazard at its worst. This fluid state of economic and legal development is as fascinating in its complexity as it is baffling in its inconsistency.

The reader will note that the dates given in this essay are those which appear in the sources consulted. No adjustment has been made of the Old Style dates of the English period, since in many cases those dates are the best index for finding materials in the manuscript collections. In referring to years, I have consistently followed the calendar year in which the date falls. Thus February 3 of the English legal year 1710-1711 becomes February 3, 1711. Any dates for the periods of Dutch occupation are of course in calendar years, and in the New Style.

I

COMMERCE OF NEW YORK

1664 TO 1730

When the flag of the States General of Holland was lowered by command of the fiery Director General Peter Stuyvesant and the city of New Amsterdam was surrendered to the forces of the duke of York, the days of Dutch settlement on the North American continent drew to a close. The Dutch citizens watching the surrender were filled with apprehensions little soothed by the leniency of the Articles of Surrender, but had they been granted the peace of mind in which to consider their previous condition the change of authority would not have appeared entirely detrimental. For four years the people of New Netherland had suffered not only political despotism but also economic hardship that reversed the prosperity of the earlier days and deprived the poor of their daily bread.

Prior to 1664 the colony at New Amsterdam served as the New World agent for the burghers of Amsterdam in Holland. When the chaotic days of the English Interregnum alienated the southern colonies of England from the mother country, the planters turned to Dutch shipping to transport their goods to European markets.[1] There was a ready market in Europe for tobacco, and large quantities were carried in the coastal trade to New Amsterdam, where Dutch trading vessels stopped to bargain for the commodity.[2] Little trade seems to have been conducted between New Amsterdam and New England, probably because of the lack of a market for European goods in that area which was well supplied from England. At the same time a lack of vessels of sufficient tonnage sharply limited any trade with the West Indies, and any Dutch trade with those islands would have been by means of the large trading ships of the Dutch West Indies Company, and not through the merchants of New Amsterdam. In a very real sense New Amsterdam was a mere New World appendage of the business community of Amsterdam, and its continued existence depended upon the trade advantages it conferred on the Dutch commercial interests. By channeling tobacco from America directly to Amsterdam the little community on the Hudson was exceeding its most optimistic expectations.

After the Restoration the pattern of trade between Virginia and New Amsterdam did not disappear, although the reenactment of the Acts of Trade and Navigation in 1660 seems to have had some restrictive effect on this trade in tobacco, which was an enumerated commodity under the acts. Not only were the Virginians reluctant to antagonize the new monarch, but it would seem that the English mercantile houses were aggressively competing with the Dutch and compliance with the acts was made less burdensome for the Virginians. The courts of New Amsterdam reacted by insisting that all contracts for the delivery of tobacco be strictly enforced despite the existence of the Acts of Trade.[3] In spite of all their efforts the prosperous times of the sixteen-fifties were past, and although tobacco remained a medium of exchange, it seems to have declined in importance in the economy of New Amsterdam.

A decline in tobacco importation due to the English Acts of Trade was a serious blow to the prosperity of New Amsterdam, but was not critical in the absence of rigorous enforcement by the English authorities.[4] At the same time the fur trade of New Netherland seems to have suffered from the competition offered by English and French factors. As competitive bidding increased the price of beaver pelts and other furs, the value of sewan[5] declined and the residents of New Amsterdam were unable to purchase goods cheaply with sewan.[6] A recommendation was made to the director general that the value of sewan be fixed annually,[7] but this measure would have been merely temporary relief unless an effective control could be reimposed on the fur trade.

The Indian tribes in the Hudson River Valley and the English colonists on Long Island caused not only military problems for the Dutch, but also accelerated the depression in the economy of New Amsterdam. Even at that early date the city on Manhattan Island was a center of commercial rather than agricultural activity, and the few garden plots in the city and beyond the *Waal* could not provide adequate sustenance for the inhabitants. To a considerable degree the city of New Amsterdam was as dependent upon the hinterland for food as its modern successor is today. Disrupted lines of transportation to the farmlands of the mid-Hudson Valley and Long Island caused a shortage in the supply of wheat and Indian corn for milling and baking in the city.[8] Even before the hostilities were under way the Burgomasters' Court had found it necessary to increase the price of bread twice within the period from March to April 1663.[9] While the standard of currency was depreciating in value the supply of wheat was decreasing, thereby creating great hardship among the poorer classes who depended upon bread as a principal ingredient of their diet.

The decline in the tobacco trade, supplemented by the inflation of sewan and the decrease in the supply of wheat and corn, created an economic condition unfavorable to the continued existence of New Netherland under the Dutch flag. Not only was life on Manhattan becoming more burdensome, but the lack of profit from the colony diminished the support which it had previously enjoyed in Holland. The conquest by the English again opened up the possibility of conducting a coastal trade in tobacco and quieted the warfare on the borders of the province, but did little to restore the province's preeminence in the fur trade. For two decades following the first English occupation in 1664 economic depression seems to have continued in New York.

A gradual establishment of trade with the West Indies brought a greater variety of goods to the New York marketplace and increased the prosperity of the town.[10] The whaling industry on Long Island provided oil for export as well as whalebone,[11] and the flour-milling monopoly was designed to bolster the sagging economy and standardize the quality of the meal exported from New York.[12] Trade in Virginia and Maryland tobacco seems to have flourished even during the brief reoccupation of New York by the Dutch in 1673 and 1674.[13] A shortage of flour in 1670 and 1673, probably due to poor harvests, caused the authorities to restrict the export of wheat in grain and in flour, thereby conserving the limited amount available to support the people of the province.[14] Since flour was one of the principal exports of the colony the export restrictions were an indication of the serious nature of the shortage,[15] and must have resulted in a severe limitation on New York's commerce.

While New Yorkers eagerly took advantage of their opportunities as members of the English empire by initiating trade with the West Indies, they were not unaware of the valuable connections they had made in Amsterdam, the financial capital of

Europe. While the merchants were unsuccessful in their attempt to obtain duty-free trade with Holland in 1668,[16] the trade with Amsterdam continued uninterrupted throughout the period under consideration. Although some of this commerce may have been perfectly legal, the likelihood is that most of the raw materials carried to Amsterdam were on the enumerated lists, and thus could be legally imported by Europeans only through English ports. Except for a few arrests of merchant ships for violations of the Acts of Trade and Navigation,[17] the Amsterdam-New York commerce appears to have been as free from government intervention as it was certain to yield profits. The retention of Dutch weights and measures,[18] and the use of the Dutch language in commercial transactions[19] seem to have survived well into the eighteenth century.

As a proprietary colony of the duke of York, and as a royal province, New York had always been subject to duties on her imports and exports, while the neighboring colonies of East and West Jersey enjoyed free trade and little supervision from proprietor or crown. As the population of the Jerseys grew, the merchants of New York were quick to notice the threat to their interests, and their mayor wrote to England suggesting that East and West Jersey be added to the territory of New York. He indicated that the city of New York had lost a third of its trade to the free ports of East Jersey and that there had been a decrease in the population of the city of New York.[20] On receipt of the letter the Committee of Trade and Plantations recommended the issuance of a *quo warranto* to annul the grant to the Jersey proprietors, but no action seems to have been taken prior to the proceedings to set up the Dominion of New England in April 1686.[21] When New Perth was created a port of entry by an order in council dated August 14, 1687, it became subject to commercial duties, and some of its advantages over New York were thereby eliminated.[22] While New Jersey may well have absorbed New York's population because of its more liberal land policy, it seems questionable whether the impact of its commercial activities on New York was as drastic as pictured by the mayor. Rather it seems that the decreased trade of New York was due to the effects of wheat shortages noted above and the competition of Boston commercial houses.[23]

While there is a general lack of evidence concerning the trade between New York and England during the seventeenth century, it seems likely that this trade was left largely to the merchants of Boston and that few New Yorkers wished to assume the risk of transatlantic trade. Those who were not content with the more secure profits of the coastal and West Indies trade could find greater profits waiting for them in Amsterdam than in London. In this regard the commercial career of Robert Livingston may be typical. For five years he traded with John Hull of Boston, and then entered the Amsterdam, London, and Barbados trade.[24] In negotiating with his London correspondent he found a marked reluctance to extend credit, which might have discouraged any New York merchant not related, as Livingston was, to the wealthy Stephanus Van Cortlandt.[25] Livingston settled his London accounts by shipments of fur pelts, but did so rather slowly, to the dismay of his creditors.[26] With his strong financial backing Livingston managed to survive his ventures into the London trade, but his difficulties indicate that many pitfalls stood in the path of the New Yorker who wished to deal directly with London.

Shortly after the turn of the century it was noted that there was little direct trade between New York and London, and that dispatches to the home government had to be sent along the coast to either Boston or Philadelphia.[27] For a brief period during King William's War (1689-1697), trade between New York and England seems to have increased because of the greater risk of French privateers in more northerly waters,[28] and in 1698 Bellomont reported that trade had doubled in the prior ten years.[29] A general prosperity came to New York between 1692 and the end of the century,[30] and it seems likely that this was partially attributable to the threat posed by privateers to the Boston-to-London trade. After the war ended, Boston seems to have resumed her place as the primary importer of English goods into North America.[31]

With their newfound wealth New York merchants entered the slave trade and sailed to Madagascar to obtain profitable human cargoes. Since this infringed upon the franchise of the Royal African Company, the home government did its best to stifle the enterprise but was able only to insure that the illegal commerce would not increase.[32] At the same time the home government was issuing instructions to curtail piracy, Colonel Benjamin Fletcher, governor of New York, achieved great popularity with his colony by entertaining pirate crews and extending a hearty welcome to them. No doubt the Act for the Encouragement of Seamen[33] was intended to give succor to all men of the sea, whether pirate, privateer, or merchantman.

The attempts by the earl of Bellomont to enforce the Acts of Trade brought great opposition from both New York merchants and their London correspondents.[34] He in turn referred to piracy and unlawful trade as the "beloved twins" of the New York merchants.[35] Despite the animosity that developed, Bellomont seems to have been concerned for the welfare of the province, for he not only requested the government to create a larger English market for furs, but also advanced plans for the production of naval stores.[36] A true advocate of mercantilism, Bellomont might have secured extended prosperity for New York had he not died at his post on March 5, 1701.[37]

Acting on Bellomont's recommendation, the Board of Trade authorized the shipment of Palatine Germans to New York for the express purpose of employing them in the production of tar and other naval stores. While some initial success in this project directed attention to America as an economical source for the raw materials desperately needed by the English navy, naval

10

stores do not seem to have occupied any considerable proportion of the exports of New York. Rather the province continued to rely heavily upon its wheat crop, which by this time had replaced furs as the primary export commodity.[38] In the future the prosperity of New York was to be sharply affected by the wheat harvest and the market conditions for wheat in the West Indies, the continental English colonies, and in Europe.[39] The importance of the wheat crop is reflected in the attempts of the provincial authorities to regulate the quality of flour exported. A reputation for high quality was maintained, but when controls were removed and the bolting of flour was opened to the general public, the West Indies planters discovered that New York flour was adulterated with Indian corn and promptly switched to flour from Pennsylvania. This was the reason given for the decline in New York's trade during the years 1694 and 1695.[40]

With the coming of Queen Anne's War the market for New York flour in the Spanish islands of the West Indies was eliminated by the embargo of the Spanish authorities.[41] At about the same time there was a surplus of agricultural produce in England,[42] and New York spent a few uncomfortable years before a wheat shortage in Europe brought renewed prosperity to the province.[43] Direct trade with the French possessions in America was rendered hazardous by the number of French privateers and English warships in American waters, but an indirect trade with the French by means of the neutral Dutch islands was maintained in such an apparent manner that the Board of Trade ordered the governor to stop the trade and to refuse to issue flags of truce, which were being misused to facilitate this provisioning.[44] After the war, Spanish authorities continued to harass New York vessels carrying provisions to the West Indies,[45] but Governor Robert Hunter was unsuccessful in prohibiting the illegal trade with the French West Indies.[46]

In exporting flour, bread, and other provisions to the southern tobacco colonies and to the West Indies, New Yorkers utilized small vessels designed for the coastal trade. There was a heavy reliance on Boston for the export of flour and for the import of manufactured goods to and from Europe,[47] at least until 1730. There can be little doubt that Boston was the queen of American commerce during the first three decades of the eighteenth century. Through their Boston correspondents New York merchants ordered rugs,[48] Madeira wines,[49] rum,[50] tallow candles,[51] and probably most of the textiles and manufactured goods not produced locally. Although such indirect trade with England partially insulated New York from the balance of payments deficit inherent in the mercantilist system, the men of commerce viewed Boston's supremacy with a jealous eye.[52]

Initial attempts at establishing direct trade with England on a large scale met with considerable difficulty because of the competitive advantages enjoyed by Bostonians.[53] Not only did Boston build her own oceangoing vessels, but she also possessed a sufficient manpower pool from which to draw seamen at relatively low wages. Despite these disadvantages, John Wick of Northampton, Long Island, entered into trade with Bristol in 1711 and successfully marketed his European goods in New York City.[54] Cadwallader Colden also found it cheaper to deal directly with London and Amsterdam merchants in purchasing books and medicines.[55] Apparently the percentage charged by Boston merchants above the cost of goods in Europe made the trade between Europe and New York a profitable one. As New York increased in financial strength her merchants entered this trade in increasing numbers.

Once Queen Anne's War ended, the pressures toward direct New York to England trade were increased by the decline of Bostonian financial stability. It is possible that some Boston merchants had entered into speculation in England, and that fortunes were lost in the crash of the speculative "bubble" of the South Seas Company in 1720. Boston also suffered from the decline in trade which followed decreased government expenditures in time

12

of peace. Yet the most likely cause for Boston's declining place in commerce was the issuance of a large number of bills of credit based upon the revenues and anticipated revenues of the provincial government.

Throughout the colonial period there was a great need for a convenient medium of exchange. Unfavorable trade balances with England were secured by the Acts of Trade and Navigation, and caused a constant drain of precious metals from the colonies.[56] All customs and quitrents were payable only in gold or silver. Because of its West Indies trade New York was able to obtain sufficient gold and silver in exchange for its wheat and other provisions, and to use this "heavy money" to settle its balances with Boston and England. For many years New York attempted with little success to retain the precious metals in the colony, but commercial necessity and political pressure from England defeated these attempts.[57] Boston, deprived of the valuable provision export trade by barren soil, apparently had less success in demanding solid coin from the foreign West Indies.

To remedy the shortage of money the colonial assemblies began to authorize the issuance of bills of credit, based upon anticipated revenues or upon the value of land in the province. As greater amounts of credit bills were issued the price of silver rose and this rise was doubtless accompanied by a hoarding of precious metals.[58] In the issuance of bills the New York Assembly seems to have exercised considerable restraint, and New York bills of credit were second only to silver and gold in stability and exchange value.[59] While the self-restraint of the Assembly enabled New York merchants to compete more successfully with Boston, it also retained a restricted amount of currency in the province and caused considerable hardship for laborers and small shopkeepers.

New York efforts to apply controls to the currency problem were far from successful in insulating the province from the effects of the empire-wide recession in business. Interest on loans began to rise because of the scarcity of money, and business, deprived of the stimulant of credit, began to decline. Imposition of a ceiling on interest rates was accomplished by an act of the Assembly in 1717, but this measure was probably designed more to obtain popular support for the incumbent assemblymen than for purposes of regulation.[60] A general decline in shipping activity occurred in the period between 1727 and 1730, and trade with Great Britain declined even more rapidly than the overall average. The proportionally greater decline in British trade indicates a desire to conserve currency, and also shows that trade with England was conducted to obtain luxury goods rather than necessities. When the colony was prospering trade with Great Britain increased in proportion to the population growth, but hard times caused sharp restrictions on the importation of goods from Britain.[61]

In 1730, as in 1664, New York was beset by economic difficulties far beyond the control of her governing authorities or her merchants.[62] The intervening years had been ones of considerable commercial development and prosperity, and the former trading post at New Amsterdam was on the verge of becoming an important port in world commerce. A barter economy had given way to one based upon credit, and the instruments for extension of credit played a growing part in the business of the city. By 1730 the city of New York was well established as one of the three major ports in colonial North America, and her future prosperity was insured by the high credit standing of the New York merchants and the abundant wheat harvests in the upriver counties.

THE DEVELOPMENT

OF THE LAW MERCHANT

Despite the changes which the late seventeenth and early eighteenth century brought to the business economy of New York City, the one invariable characteristic was its commitment to oceanic commerce as the primary source of wealth. With enterprise so directed it is not surprising that a large part of the litigation before the provincial courts concerned commercial transactions. To a large degree the commercial advancement of the city from 1664 to 1730 was due to the ostensibly effortless transformation from a system of Dutch civil law to one of English common law.[1] Such a fundamental change in the law could have had devastating effects on the business community, which relies heavily upon fixed relationships between parties and a standardization of business procedures.

While it is certain that the gradual nature of the change in the legal system of New York was in part due to the reluctance of the English conquerors to arouse resistance through imposing new laws on a predominantly Dutch population, there can be no doubt that the easy transition from the Dutch law to the English law was greatly facilitated by the developments which had taken place in English law and its reception of the law merchant into the common law. It is only after considering the nature of those developments that one becomes aware of their importance to the early legal history of the province of New York. After nearly a century of rapid change, English common law had absorbed most of the law merchant and by 1664 was reasonably close to the system of commercial law described by Hugo Grotius in his *The Jurisprudence of Holland.*[2]

The law merchant developed in England and in the Netherlands from a variety of local customs and uses. Finally evolved into a group of generally accepted traditions, the custom received the support of legal sanction and became a personal law that accompanied the merchant on his travels.[3] This personal law of the trading class, enforced in courts of mercantile origin, is the basis for the modern law merchant. Limited though it was in applying only to members of the community of merchants, it carried within it the capacity for expansion to include the entire scope of commercial activity. Indeed the very adaptability of the English common law to modern business transactions is due in no small degree to the reception of the law merchant during the early seventeenth century.[4]

Sweeping northward from the Mediterranean, the influence of Eastern trade was gradually felt in the isolated agricultural kingdom of England by the end of the eleventh century. At first the luxuries and technological inventions of the East were the sole concern of the royal household, and it is not strange that the king

16

was foremost in the encouragement of foreign trade. Yet the agrarian occupation of the people of England left the field of commerce bereft of English participants, and the king was forced to offer valuable inducements to encourage the settlement of foreign merchants on English soil for the purpose of carrying on trade with the continent. As early as 1291 complaints of merchants were heard by the king and proof was given according to the law merchant.[5] Sixty-two years later, foreign merchants were given the privilege to hold their own Courts of the Staple according to merchant customs, and only pleas of felony and freehold were withheld from these courts.[6] Further concessions may be found in the precept that the arrest of a foreign merchant could be obtained only after showing that the party wronged could not obtain redress at the place where the wrong occurred,[7] and that courts in the towns were required to render judgment on the same day that causes affecting foreign merchants were presented to them.[8] At the beginning of the sixteenth century we may well say that the foreign merchant occupied an enviable position in the realm of England, and that he enjoyed numerous advantages over his English associates.[9]

Early English custom had recognized the right of traders at trading fairs to settle their disputes in Courts of the Fair, which came to be known as "piepoudre courts" because of the flour-covered footwear of the litigants. In 1477 the jurisdiction of these courts was restricted to causes arising at the time and place of the fair,[10] thereby leaving the enforcement of the English law merchant to the courts of the trading towns, among which the most influential was the Mayor's Court of the city of London.[11] The number of foreign litigants in the London Mayor's Court and the existence of the Courts of the Staple created a strong continental bias in the law merchant that accentuated the differences between the law merchant and that of the common-law courts.

While England entered the sixteenth century a weak maritime power dependent upon foreign vessels to carry her imports and far too few exports,[12] we find her at the end of the century defeating the Armada of Philip II and starting her explorations in the New World. A robust dynasty had succeeded to the throne that had been sorely shaken by the feudal War of the Roses, and under the Tudors England became the best of all possible worlds for the native English merchant. While the rise in English-owned ships reduced the dependence upon the fleets of the Venetian commercial houses,[13] pressure was brought to bear upon the foreign merchant staplers through the efforts of Elizabeth I. The stalwart representatives of the Hanse League withstood the royal demands until 1578, at which time their privileges were canceled. They were expelled in the following year, and in 1580 the extraterritorial jurisdiction of the Steelyard, the last staple area in England, was surrendered to the political rule of the City of London.[14] This eliminated the Courts of the Staple from the realm of England, compelling merchants to resort to the town courts or the strictly limited Courts of the Fair.

The intimate relationship between maritime law and modern commercial law has been noted by Sir William S. Holdsworth, who cites as similarities the dependence of both systems upon custom and the international nature of both systems.[15] It might be added that both maritime law and the law merchant take their origin in civil rather than common law, and that both utilize exceptionally prompt procedures to secure to the complainant his satisfied judgment.[16] For these reasons it is obvious why the merchant class of England favored the rapid expansion of the jurisdiction of the High Court of Admiralty into the areas encompassed by the law merchant. With its ready recourse to civil law and the customs of the merchants, the Court of Admiralty became the principal forum of the law merchant during the Tudor period, and we find Queen Elizabeth herself objecting to the Mayor's Court of London that it infringed upon admiralty jurisdiction by trying a case arising beyond the seas.[17] At the height of its civil jurisdiction, the Court of Admiralty heard all

18

causes relating to commercial contracts, bills of exchange, commercial agencies, insurance contracts made outside the realm of England, and every other form of shipping business.[18]

The High Court of Admiralty had long been the sole recourse when the case to be tried was based upon acts taking place outside of the realm of England.[19] An unsuccessful attempt to pass a statute making a foreign charter party triable at common law was defeated in the House of Lords in 1539,[20] and there seem to have been no other attempts to extend the power of common-law courts beyond cases arising within England. By means of a fictitious pleading, the English lawyers finally established a venue in England, thereby conferring jurisdiction upon the English court.[21] Only the High Court of Admiralty was not restricted in jurisdiction by the need that the venue of the action be laid in England.

In the common-law courts of the sixteenth and early seventeenth centuries the term "venue" was nearly equivalent to "jurisdiction." Venue was not only the neighborhood from which the trial jury was drawn, but it was also the place where the injury occurred, and the determination of whether any local customs would apply also depended upon the venue of the action at law.[22] In a system of justice in which the jury was still a panel of witnesses to the occurrence, the strict rules of venue provided a guarantee that knowledgeable men would try the issue.[23] By the end of the sixteenth century the jury no longer served this purpose, and frequent recourse was had to sworn witnesses; the jury had become the trier rather than the supplier of the facts. Although venue as a prerequisite of jurisdiction had considerable validity in a land-oriented economy with a witness jury system, it was an unhealthy restraint on the growth of the law in an economy based on movable property with a trial jury system.

In the practice before the Mayor's Court of London we find some indication that the venue tradition of the common-law courts had taken root in that traditionally mercantile forum.[24]

Yet in the constitution of the jury the court was not bound to draw all jurors from the vicinity in which the venue was laid.[25] Through the use of a jury of merchants from another market-place, the court was rendered capable of trying causes which arose at that marketplace, and in applying the local customs of that town rather than the customs of London.[26] In this manner the Mayor's Court combined the venue system of the common law with the more sweeping *in personam* jurisdiction that was exercised in the High Court of Admiralty.

Not only did venue confer jurisdiction on the common-law court, it also supplied the substantive law that would decide the case. In many instances this would be the common law of England, in a few the customary law of the vicinity, but in no case could an English court of common law take any cognizance of the law of another sovereign state.[27] Authorities differ on the precise time when this refusal to recognize foreign law gave way to an attempt to apply the *jus gentium*, or common private law of all nations, and thereby insure a uniform enforcement of duties and obligations no matter what national forum was called upon to decide the issues in a given case. The recognition of rules that will determine what body of law will apply to a given event is the basis for a system of conflicts of law, which in turn provides for the universal recognition of rights which is vital to the protection of international trade. Because of the international character of the law merchant it is not unlikely that the first elements of a system of conflicts of laws was introduced into common law when the common law received the law merchant into its fabric.[28]

A concept of conflicts of law was not the only void which the merchant community found in the common law after the attack of Sir Edward Coke eliminated the Court of Admiralty from the enforcement of the law merchant in all causes arising upon land. At the time of the accession of James I it is clear that bills of exchange, policies of insurance, and the free assignability of debts were unknown to the common law.[29] The prompt procedures for attaching the goods or arresting the person of a debtor were not available at common law until after the plaintiff had exhausted his procedural remedies through intermediate process. This procedure was not only expensive, but it was time-consuming and totally ineffective in an economy based upon movable rather than fixed property.

These, and many other encumbrances on common-law procedure and substantive law, created a need for rapid assimilation of the law merchant into the common law of England. This development took place gradually before the decline of admiralty jurisdiction during the reign of James I, but the reception of merchant customs was greatly accelerated during the six decades preceding the conquest of New York in 1664. By that time we may say that most of the law merchant was enforceable in the courts of common law as well as in the merchant courts. Perhaps the sole exception to this overall reception was the free assignability of debts, and this will form the subject matter of the two chapters dealing with the history of negotiable instruments in the province of New York.

An ancient prohibition against the practice of maintenance had caused the rule that debts owing to a subject could not be assigned by him to another subject, but only to the king. The intent of the prohibition was to discourage one not originally involved in the suit from obtaining part of the proceeds of the judgment. The initially desirable effect of discouraging lawsuits had been far offset by the inability of creditors to rediscount their advances through other moneylenders, and sorely crippled the development of an economy based on credit. By the turn of the seventeenth century the demand for a change in England became critical, and New York was fast approaching a state in which such a change in its laws would be needed. In New York, as in England, the courts were receptive to the needs of the commercial community and reacted promptly to the new conditions under which business was to be conducted.

THE LAW MERCHANT

IN NEW YORK COLONIAL COURTS

Prior to the English conquest the Dutch inhabitants of New Amsterdam could boast of a highly developed system of jurisprudence based upon the laws and customs of the Netherlands. Their Court of Burgomasters, Schepens, and Schout was established in 1653 when the city of New Amsterdam had been incorporated.[1] It exercised a broad jurisdiction encompassing nearly every conceivable type of litigation, and was subject to review only by the court held intermittently by the director general and his council. Because of the great amount of causes referred to the Burgomasters' Court, it was found expedient to form a court for the supervision of orphan apprentices as an inferior tribunal.

With this single exception all other civil controversies and prosecutions for crimes were heard in the Burgomasters' Court.

Beyond the limits of New Amsterdam small local courts of magistrates performed the same functions as the Burgomasters' Court, and in the patroonship of Rensselaerswyck the feudal courts constituted the sole refuge of the tenants. Over all of these tribunals the director general and his council exercised a general appellate jurisdiction.

Practice in the Dutch courts was patterned closely after that of the mother country,[2] as were the laws and customs which were enforced.[3] However, the informality bred by frontier life had made its mark upon the courts, for in the Burgomasters' Court it was commonplace for a party to fail to appear before the judges, even after being formally summoned.[4] When the litigants did appear they usually pleaded their cause in person and rarely submitted written pleadings. As the weight of litigation forced the court to place limitations on this impromptu justice, the role of the notary public grew in importance as he was called upon to draw up the pleadings in proper form and to appear for his clients. At the time of the English conquest there were about nine notaries in New Amsterdam.[5]

Under the English little effort was made to alter the court system of New Netherland. The Duke's Laws, a comprehensive codification of the laws that would apply to the province, set up a General Court of Assizes which was to be composed of the governor, his council, the high sheriff, and such justices of the peace as might choose to attend.[6] While the Duke's Laws were only gradually extended to New Amsterdam proper they did not work any considerable change on its judicial system. The effect of the law was merely to change the composition of the court exercising appellate review over the Burgomasters' Court. Fundamentally the Court of Assizes did not differ from the old court of the director general and his council. The Burgomasters' Court continued with only a name change in 1665 to conform to English usage.[7]

In 1684 the Court of Assizes was abolished by an act of the newly formed General Assembly, and was succeeded by the Court of Chancery. The latter court served as supreme court until 1688 when it was briefly succeeded by the Superior Court of the Dominion of New England. Courts of Oyer and Terminer served as appellate courts from 1688 until the creation of the Supreme Court of Judicature by an act of the Assembly in 1691.[8] Since only fragmentary records remain concerning appellate courts before the Supreme Court of Judicature it is difficult to determine whether they played any significant role in the development of the law merchant. We can only surmise that in exercising supervisory authority over the Mayor's Court they did not restrict it in its application of the law merchant, nor did they exact strict compliance with English common law.[9]

By 1691 the need for a court with nisi prius and en banc terms became too pressing to be ignored, and the Supreme Court of Judicature was designed to meet this requirement.[10] The physical hardship of riding the circuit and the small allowances made for the judges while on circuit resulted in but little nisi prius litigation.[11] Most of the cases before the Supreme Court were either real property actions or criminal prosecutions, but it was empowered to hear all causes where the damages or amount in controversy exceeded £20.[12] While it was possible for cases involving the law merchant to be presented to the Supreme Court for trial, it is likely that most cases in the mercantile area came before the Supreme Court on appeal.[13]

The Vice-admiralty Court of the Province of New York exercised the closely limited judicial power of the High Court of Admiralty in England.[14] The traditional conflict between common law and admiralty law was well known in the province, and little conflict with the Supreme Court of Judicature seems to have developed.[15] Concurrent jurisdiction existed with the Supreme Court of Judicature in cases involving violations of the Acts of Trade and Navigation, the Supreme Court deriving its powers from its grant of Exchequer jurisdiction.[16] The existing records of the Vice-admiralty Court from 1715 to 1730 indicate that its business consisted mainly of criminal prosecutions for breaches of the Acts of Trade, and settlements of claims to vessels and cargoes taken as prizes by privateers.[17] Because of the limited scope of the Vice-admiralty Court it is doubtful that it influenced the enforcement of the law merchant in New York.

An interesting act of the Assembly provided for the creation of Courts of the Fair in New York and designated the mayor of New York City as governor of any fairs that might be held in the city.[18] As had been noted previously the English piepoudre courts had been severely limited in jurisdiction, and the courts envisaged by the act were also limited to the time and place of the fair. So limited in power, the piepoudre courts in England continued well into the eighteenth century,[19] and we may consider the existence of such New York courts during this period as in accordance with the laws of England. It would seem that the piepoudre courts erected in New York were not courts of record, and like the manorial courts established in the province, we cannot tell whether they ever functioned because of the lack of records. Any contribution which the piepoudre courts made to the law merchant must have been negligible.

As in England, the most effective vehicle for the development of the law merchant into a modern system of commercial law was the Mayor's Court. Just as English commerce centered in London and gave preeminence to the Mayor's Court of London, so did New York's economy dictate that the New York City Mayor's Court assume a position of leadership in mercantile litigation. Fortunately there is available a complete record of the litigation before this court, and before its predecessor, the Dutch Court of Burgomasters, Schepens, and Schout. The wealth of information contained in this vast manuscript record bears eloquent testimony of the importance of the New York Mayor's Court to the administration of justice in the province.[20]

The transition from Burgomasters' Court to Mayor's Court was accomplished with few changes in the procedure of the court. Most significant was the introduction of the jury system, an institution unknown to Dutch jurisprudence.[21] Except for the brief period during which the Dutch held the province in 1673 and 1674, the jury remained a part of Mayor's Court procedure. After the indictment of members of the court for failure to allow a trial by jury, there could be little doubt of the popularity of this innovation.[22] While a reorganization of the court was made in the Dongan charter of 1686,[23] the attempt to relieve the dockets of the courts was rather unsuccessful and the number of causes adjourned seems to have increased with the years. As the jurisdictional amount of the court was fixed at a minimum of forty shillings in 1672, and never increased up to 1730, the reason for crowded dockets is fairly obvious.[24]

As early as January of 1670 the Mayor's Court found it necessary to instruct litigants to employ attorneys-at-law to "Bring the Controversy to a narrow Composure."[25] Yet the number of trained lawyers in the province at that time was small, and of that number few were members of the Inns of Court.[26] Not until the last decade of the seventeenth century did pleading through attorneys become commonplace in the Mayor's Court,[27] and a degree of informality of procedure persisted until that time. The three barristers in the province in 1691 were joined by ten more by 1701.[28] Both the members of the Inns of Court and their less formally trained associates at the bar found practice before the Mayor's Court profitable. Popular pressure to reduce attorney's fees was countered by the formation of a bar association in 1709 and 1710,[29] and in 1731 eight lawyers were successful in obtaining a temporary monopoly over practice in the Mayor's Court;[30] an indication of the value which attorneys placed upon practice in that court.

Although the influx of lawyers trained at the English Inns of Court brought with it much of the formalism of English pleading,[31] the Mayor's Court remained a distinctly mercantile forum. Arrest, attachment, and arbitration continued to play a vital part in its procedure. In the receipt of account books in evidence, and in its treatment of suits brought by married women, it reflected the influence of the law merchant. At times it recognized the laws and mercantile customs of foreign nations, but it nevertheless clung to a venue system based upon fictitious pleadings.[32] Thoroughly Anglicized by the eighteenth century, it represented that peculiar blend of merchant custom and English common law characteristic of English mercantile courts of that day.

While the increasing number of English barristers practicing in the province of New York resulted in a closer adherence to English legal traditions, it did not impede the application of the law merchant. One reason for this was the advanced state of the reception of the law merchant into common law by the end of the seventeenth century. In those areas where the enforceability of mercantile law was questionable it would seem that the slow growth of New York's economy during the seventeenth century made it unnecessary for provincial law to advance beyond the English law of the day. This was particularly true in the case of promissory notes, which will be discussed in the following chapter, for here English financial needs caused a change in the law long before a similar need existed in New York.[33]

The courts of the province of New York were following the English lead in their application of the law merchant, but the lack of departure from the English standard was not due to a slavish reproduction of English law. Rather the needs of the merchants were not of such a nature that rapid growth was required, and innovations usually flowed from England to New York, from a well-developed economy to a newborn commercial and financial center. While the courts would ultimately determine the law merchant applicable in New York, their action could only be predicated upon the financial needs of the commercial community of the province.

WRITTEN EVIDENCES OF DEBT

AND PROMISSORY NOTES

All commercial enterprise thrives upon a constant diet of paper, pen, and ink; in the account book, the contract, the letter, and the memorandum, the businessman faithfully records his progress toward the opulence of success or the degradation of bankruptcy. Just as a certain finality and perpetuity attach to the written word, so does a certain aura of sanctity attach to the personal signature, and the man who would hasten to deny his oral agreements takes pause when an agreement in writing bears his autograph. If credit be "Man's Faith in Man," then the written evidences of debt are the most effective insurance that that faith rarely shall be shaken.[1]

The Dutch at New Amsterdam were well aware of the value of written evidence of debts, and despite the barter nature of their economy they had a highly systematized body of law concerning the use of formal writings obligatory. While these formal documents seem to have been the principal evidence of debt used in New Amsterdam, there is some evidence that informal writings were also used for this purpose.[2] The absence of any consistent record of the informal writings obligatory may be explained by the very nature of the instrument. Not only was it for such a small amount of money or goods that the expense of formal execution was unwarranted, but the informal obligation was also executed by persons of lesser estate who needed such small sums, and they were less likely to preserve the obligation after the debt had been repaid. Furthermore, it will be noted that most of the evidence concerning the formal obligation has been found in notarial registers, the records of notaries public who prepared and witnessed the formal obligations. For these reasons it is impossible to determine the state of the law on informal writings obligatory during the last years of the Dutch occupation.

The formal obligation in writing was executed by the debtor in the presence of a notary public and two other witnesses.[3] After the obligor affixed his signature or mark, the witnesses and the notary signed the instrument and it was recorded in the notary public's register.[4] Frequently the creditor was present and accepted the obligation in the presence of the notary and other witnesses.[5] Married women could sign obligations on their own behalf, and could also sign obligations that would be binding upon their husbands.[6] The basis in fact for the issuance of the obligation was always expressed in the instrument, but a gratuitous maker of an obligation for the sole benefit of another was held to be liable for the repayment of the money advanced to that other.[7] It was also customary to express the property which would be forfeited to the creditor if the obligation remained unpaid at the due date. While the expression of the security posted seems to have conveyed to the creditor some interest in that property, the recitation of the underlying business transaction was probably set forth to preclude any dispute concerning the agreement.[8] Obligations were executed for a large variety of purposes and were payable in either commodities or current money.[9] For each obligation which he drafted, and subsequently witnessed, the notary public received a fee.[10] A fee was also received whenever a duplicate copy of the obligation was issued by him to replace one lost or destroyed.[11]

Under Dutch law all debts were assignable, and the formal obligation was transferred with all of the precautions that attended its execution.[12] The entire debt represented by the obligation could be assigned, or only a certain part of the debt could be transferred while the creditor retained the other part to himself.[13] An assignee took the obligation subject to all of the defenses that might be interposed against his assignor, and was held to settle all existing accounts between his assignor and the obligor before proceeding with a suit to recover on the obligation.[14] At times the creditor would instruct the obligor to pay the amount due to an agent, but there is no indication that such an agent could bring an action based upon the obligation unless it had been conveyed to him before a notary and two witnesses.[15]

In a suit upon a written contract, provisional payment by the promissor was required, and pending the receipt of evidence the promissor's property could be attached to secure the judgment.[16] A necessary prerequisite to bringing suit on an obligation was that the failure to perform according to the terms of the instrument be made the subject of a timely protest to the defaulting party.[17] In presenting his case to the court, the creditor, or his assignee, was required to produce the original obligation or a notarial copy of the destroyed original obligation.[18]

While fraud in the making of the obligation was possible as a defense, the formal procedure of execution and the terms of the instrument itself made it unlikely that the obligor had been tricked into signing his name.[19] The strongest defense available was that of payment of all or part of the debt, and the courts were liberal in admitting proof on this allegation.[20] It can be seen that the party who brought suit on a formal instrument had a distinct advantage because the obligation itself was strong evidence against fraud, expressed the exact amount due and the transaction underlying the debt, indicated the security provided for the plaintiff's satisfaction, and provided three witnesses to the execution.

The coming of the English made as little immediate change in the commercial law of the province as it did in the court structure. Public policy dictated a reduction of the interest rate from the ten percent of the Dutch to the six percent legal rate imposed by the English statute.[21] The Duke's Laws, promulgated in 1665 and applied to New Amsterdam in 1669, specifically provided that debts evidenced by "Specialtyes" would be assignable, thereby continuing the assignability of formal obligations but leaving the situation in doubt concerning informal evidences of debt.[22] At this time in England neither specialties nor obligations nor informal notes were assignable except to or by the king.[23]

A gradual change took place in the formalities required for the execution of an obligation, and by 1669 the English practice of execution by signing and sealing in the presence of witnesses was the acceptable method.[24] There was a growing use of the informal obligation, the forerunner of the promissory note, but the little evidence available would indicate that the informal obligation was not assignable.[25] A form of penal bill began to be used, but it does not seem to have been at all important during the decade following the English conquest.[26] The continued use of the formal obligation and the advanced position taken in regard to assignability by the Duke's Laws make the change from Dutch to English law nearly imperceptible. Were it not for the growing importance of informal obligations and the introduction of the penal bill, the decade would be singularly uneventful.

The last quarter of the seventeenth century was one of civil disorder and wartime frenzy in the province of New York. Were it not for the unsettled political conditions it is possible that the pressure toward acceptance of the common law would have been stronger. Those changes which took place in the law-of-debt writings obligatory indicate that the English standard was being followed to a greater degree as the years passed, and the arrival of the English-trained lawyers at the end of the seventeenth century merely accelerated this process.

One of the aspects in which English practice seems to have been accepted was in the admission of personal defenses against the holder of a formal obligation. In Dutch times and during the English occupation under Nicolls and Lovelace, the only defenses available to the party sued on a formal obligation were payment or the ability to prove fraud in obtaining the execution of the note.[27] With the elimination of the requirement that the formal obligation be executed before a notary public, the number of defenses based on the ground of fraudulent inducement increased. By 1680 the Court of Assizes reversed a judgment of the Mayor's Court for the holder of a sealed obligation after determining that the maker of the obligation had a valid personal defense. In this case the maker of the obligation had purchased a Negro slave who, according to the warranty of the obligee, was in good health. The Negro died shortly thereafter and the court held that the obligation was unenforceable against the purchaser.[28] This decision would seem to conform to the English practice of permitting proof of the underlying consideration in a suit on an obligation.[29]

The allowance of a defense based upon the underlying transaction, while desirable from a debtor's point of view, would tend to make the obligation less transferable in the business community. Since the assignee of an obligation took it subject to all defenses that might be raised against his assignor, it was now essential that he inform himself concerning all of the details of the transaction upon which the formal obligation was based. By the end of the seventeenth century it would seem that the formal obligation no longer had the desirable characteristics of transferability that it possessed under the Dutch civil law.

Perhaps it was the increased difficulty of proving a case based upon a formal writing obligatory that caused the business community to turn to the penal-bill form of writing obligatory. It is possible that the innovation was made to enable moneylenders to circumvent the effect of the usury statutes of England, which had been extended to New York by judicial use shortly after the conquest in 1664. A scarcity of money will produce high interest rates in the absence of control by the government, and there was far too little currency in New York throughout the colonial period. Whatever the reason, the growing use of obligations expressing a penal amount to be forfeited on failure of obligor to make timely satisfaction of his debt, indicates the determination of creditors to obtain additional security for the advance of their funds. Despite pleas of defense based upon the English Usury Act of 1660,[30] and many pleas bringing the inequity of the forfeiture to the attention of the courts,[31] no relief was given to the New York debtor class until the act of the Assembly in 1730.[32]

The most significant development in this area of the law during the seventeenth century was the act of the Assembly passed on October 23, 1684, which provided that

> . . . any Debt or Debts due upon bonds or other Specialtyes or any other note in writing for any Debt Duty Demand matter or thing assigned to any other person . . . shall be as good and effectual . . . to the assignee . . . as they . . . were [to the assignor at the time of the assignment];

but that to be effective the assignment would have to be made in writing on the reverse side of the bond, specialty, or note involved.[33] It should be noted that the act substantially restated the provisions of the Duke's Laws, with a significant addition of "notes in writing" within the enumerated assignable evidences of debt. Furthermore, it provided for a form of endorsement, which had been used by the Dutch to indicate a collecting agent for a formal obligation,[34] and required that the endorsement be made in the presence of one witness or acknowledged by the assignee before a judge.[35] Such a liberal policy on the assignability of evidences of debt was not attained in England until 1704.[36]

Because this legislation was so far in advance of the law of England, it is difficult to understand why it was not annulled as being contrary to the common law. From all available records it is impossible to tell whether the act was ever forwarded to England, or whether it was ever considered by the Privy Council. The likelihood is that it never left the province of New York, for it is not mentioned in any of the official correspondence of the governor, nor in the records of the Lords of Trade, nor in the acts of the Privy Council. In the confusion attendant upon the proprietor's accession to the throne and the creation of the Dominion of New England, the act of the General Assembly of New York must have been forgotten.

Economic and legal reasons combined to limit the significance of the act of 1684 for the future development of negotiable-instrument law in New York. While some debt instruments are assigned because they are deemed uncollectable, the vast majority of assignments are made for the purpose of rediscount.[37] The financial dependence of New York upon Boston and the unfavorable balance of trade with England caused a constant flow of currency out of New York, thereby decreasing the funds available to finance business. Until the beginning of the eighteenth century, New York was a commercial community and all of its financing was carried on by its merchants. Once the merchants increased in wealth and were able to engage in the loan of surplus funds, the need for transferable evidences of indebtedness became as obvious in New York as it had been in England. The economic state of New York in 1684 would indicate no need for such a legislative act, and it seems that the commercial community ignored its provisions concerning the "note in writing" and continued to use the obligation that had been executed with the usual formalities.

While practical reasons limited the immediate effect of the act of 1684, later advantages from the act were lost by a strange inability of the legal profession to discern the New York law before 1691. It seems to have been the rule that the decisions of courts were binding only after the opening of the Supreme Court of Judicature in that year, and acts of the Assembly were binding only if enacted after the legislative session that convened in that year.[38] While such an attitude may be justified concerning the chaotic years from 1689 to 1691, it is scarcely reasonable for the years from 1664 to 1688. A final appeal to the more liberal Dutch tradition, the act of 1684 seems to have died out of memory because of the apathy of the merchants and the self-serving forgetfulness of legal purists.

It will be noted at this point that the use of the formal writing obligatory had not changed to any considerable degree since the time of the Dutch, and its continuance was due not only to its commercial value, but also to the fact that its features of assignability were not unduly distasteful to English law which was rapidly approaching a position where specialties would be assignable. On the other hand, the informal writing obligatory was used rarely, if at all, in the province of New York.[39]

A radical change was made in the law of the province by the English Promissory Note Act of 1704,[40] which declared that the reason for its enactment was that notes in writing were not assignable under the custom of merchants, and should be so assignable for the benefit of trade and commerce in the realm of England. The statute did not mention the colonies in its provisions, nor is there any indication that colonial possessions were included in its scope. Nevertheless, it is clear that the statute went into effect on May 1, 1705, and by April 22, 1709, a suit on a "certain Note in Writing" was brought in the New York Mayor's Court and in the pleadings the party alleged that he was "having Commerce" with the defendant at the time the note was executed.[41] Many suits thereafter specifically allege the existence of the statute,[42] and such an assertion was part of the forms for pleading assembled by Joseph Murray.[43]

Up to 1730 the growth in the use of promissory notes was gradual, and they never replaced the formal obligation as the most acceptable evidence of debt. Notes were used for relatively small debts and were assigned at an early date after their introduction into New York.[44] Unlike the formula for pleading on a dishonored bill of exchange, the pleading on a promissory note merely mentioned the custom of merchants, that the parties were "having Commerce," and that the note was made in accordance with the provisions of the statute.[45] Occasionally an allegation was made that the defendant fraudulently designed to deceive the plaintiff, but the rationale for this inclusion seems to have been to state a cause of action in assumpsit as well as on the note.[46] As in the case of formal obligations, disputed issues of fact were determined by a jury unless the parties consented to accept a decision of the court.[47]

In the year 1730 promissory notes were well established in the law of New York, but their use was limited by the old attachment of merchants to the formal writing obligatory. A note would suffice for the poor mariner wishing to borrow a shilling or two, but the businessman who wished a loan of one hundred pounds had to be willing to affix his seal of wax and call his witnesses. Lest we upbraid the lawyers and merchants of the eighteenth century as reactionaries we should recall that the legal effect of the seal on an instrument persisted in the state of New York until 1941,[48] and it still exists in some other jurisdictions.[49] The law changes slowly indeed, but human nature is even more immutable in the face of change. It is the human factor that governed the acceptance of the unsealed instrument after 1730.

V

NEW YORK BILLS OF EXCHANGE

One of the most spectacular developments in the English common law during the first half of the seventeenth century was the rapid acceptance of the bill of exchange into the body of English common law. As has been previously discussed, much of this absorption of the law merchant was caused by the limitation of admiralty jurisdiction by the courts of common law. The rising power of the commercial community enabled them to bring strong pressures to bear on the judges to accept the principles of the law merchant. It is clear that by 1664 the law concerning bills of exchange was fully absorbed into the common law, and for this reason there was little significant difference between the laws of England and those of Holland in regard to bills of exchange. Unlike the promissory note and its predecessor, the informal writing obligatory, there was no development of the law concerning the bill of exchange in New York. From 1664 to 1730 a degree of change in the drafting of bills occurred due more to commercial convenience than to legal necessity.

As a convenient means for settling trade balances and instruments for extending credit, the bill of exchange occupied an important part in maritime trade. It may be said without exaggeration that all trade in the Western world depended upon the use of the bill of exchange. Yet there is a strange lack of material on bills of exchange in the early court records of the province of New York that can be explained only by a reference to the trade patterns of the province as discussed heretofore. It will be recalled that there was a deficit in trade balances in regard to Great Britain and that such a situation probably existed in regard to Boston, from whence New York obtained most of its manufactured goods. An unfavorable balance of payments produces a lack of trade balances in the area to which the currency gravitates; for this reason New York merchants never had substantial sums of money on deposit with their correspondents in Europe or Boston. Bills of exchange are merely orders to one in custody of another's funds, to pay a part of those funds to a party designated by the owner of the funds. The lack of New York funds held by merchants in Boston and London severely limited the number of bills of exchange that New York merchants could draw. Therefore, an extremely small number of bills issued by New York merchants were protested because of the failure of the drawee to pay according to the order. These protested bills were the ones which found their way back to New York; upon their arrival, the purchaser of each bill of exchange sued the drawer for the amount of money payable according to its terms.

Those bills of exchange that survive from this period evidence a wide disparity of knowledge concerning the English

mode of execution. We have a chatty note from Margaret Sylvester, recently widowed, to her friend and legal advisor, Henry
Lloyd,[1] and a fairly detailed bill of exchange drawn by John
Wick, the Long Island merchant who instituted trade with Bristol
in 1710.[2] Before the conquest Dutch bills of exchange were
faithful copies of the detailed bills drawn in the Old World, and
the simplicity of the early English bills may be additional proof
of the coastal character of New York's trade during the seventeenth century.

Despite the variations in form, all bills of exchange seem
to have been satisfactory if they expressed a mandate for the payment of money. Frequent loss of vessels at sea, and the resulting
destruction of bills of exchange, caused merchants to draw their
bills in three parts and send them on different vessels.[3] Actually,
three identical bills were drawn and designated first, second, and
third bills. Upon the presentation of any part, the other parts not
being paid, the presenter would be paid and the bill considered
canceled. There is no evidence concerning the legal rights of one
who purchased one part of a bill of exchange, but who was refused payment on the ground that another part had already been
paid. Since the three-part nature of the bill was expressed in its
terms, the likelihood is that such a purchaser would be unsuccessful in obtaining payment of his partial bill.

New York bills of exchange served a variety of purposes,[4]
and their tenor, or terms of payment, ranged from sight to forty
days sight.[5] Like bills of exchange in England, they were subject
to the formal rules of presentment, protest, and notice of dishonor.[6] More than adequate time was given to the holder of a
dishonored bill in which to comply with these formalities, and
a six-year interval between time of dishonor and service of notice
of dishonor was allowed by the New York Mayor's Court.[7]

While a bill drawn payable on sight is usually presented
for payment, a bill payable a specified time after sight is as a
rule presented for acceptance. Upon the return of the bill to its

owner after nonacceptance or nonpayment, the holder was entitled to recover a premium in addition to the principal amount of the bill. During the eighteenth century a premium of twenty percent of the value of the bill of exchange was applied.[8] This premium was designed to compensate the holder of the bill for the additional expenses incidental to the formalities or protest and notice of dishonor, and also as a punitive measure against the party so defaulting in payment.[9] It was probably ancient in origin and reflects the general attitude of the community of merchants in condemning such defaults in payment.

While most suits on bills of exchange were brought against the maker by the original purchaser of the bill, there is sufficient basis for the conclusion that a party who obtained the bill through endorsement could also institute suit.[10] At times a party entitled to bring suit found it necessary to designate a representative to institute suit through the use of a letter of attorney.[11] It was also well established that once a drawee accepted the bill of exchange, he could be sued on his failure to pay, despite the fact that he had received later instructions from the drawer to refuse payment.[12] These rules were generally applied throughout England and Europe, and therefore represent no innovation on standard practice by the courts or merchants of New York.

While written evidences of indebtedness underwent considerable change during the years from 1664 to 1730, the amount of change in the laws applying to the bill of exchange is negligible. Similarity between Dutch and English practice made the transfer of political authority of little importance to the practices relating to bills of exchange. Rapid developments in English law before the occupation of New York left little if any room for legal changes thereafter. Only changes in draftsmanship are evident during the English period and we may safely claim that the bill of exchange possessed all of its modern attributes by 1664, and continued to have these characteristics throughout the colonial history of New York.

POSTSCRIPT—1730 AND AFTER

After 1730 the development of negotiable instruments law appears to consist of slight refinements upon rules and practices evolved earlier. Just as the absorption of the law merchant into the common law precluded evolution of the bill of exchange after the conquest of New York, so did the reception into New York of the English statute of 1704 prevent any substantial developments concerning the promissory note.

A certain continuity characterizes the drafting of negotiable instruments and bills obligatory, although a few changes were introduced for the protection of moneylenders.[1] Clauses confessing judgment, which authorized any New York attorney to appear on the debtor's behalf to admit the existence of the debt, began to appear about 1765.[2] Joint notes became popular at an earlier date because each of the makers became jointly and severally liable to the payee.[3]

Litigation involving negotiable instruments became less expensive as the lengthy allegations of mercantile custom were eliminated. Attorneys utilized a form of pleading prepared by scriveners, leaving space for the attorney to insert the facts particular to his client's cause.[4] In the case of pleadings on promissory notes the tendency seemed to be that the statute of 1704 was specifically pleaded as the basis of recovery.[5]

Writings obligatory continued to be the most popular form of debt security, although promissory notes secured debts of increasing magnitude. Two interesting instances of the uses of writings or bills obligatory appear in the post-1730 period. On August 13, 1760 a bond was executed by young Peter Betts and his father. Young Betts was about to be apprenticed, and his new master feared the youth's devotion to learning the trade might be weakened by the appeals of His Majesty's recruiting officers. Consequently he requested and received a bond conditioned upon the boy's completing the four years and six months of apprenticeship without enlisting in the army or the provincial militia. In the event the call to arms proved too strong, the father would be obliged to pay the master the sum of £11.[6]

Another example of the use of a penal bill in the field of education occurs in a post-Revolutionary manuscript which possibly reflects a long-standing collegiate practice. When David Jones entered Columbia College in 1792 his father, Samuel Jones, was required to join with him in executing a bond in the amount of £200, conditioned upon the payment of all tuition fees by the young gentleman. So routine was the transaction that the trustees provided a printed form for this purpose![7]

The growth of British power in North America is reflected in the variety of uses of the bill of exchange. During the "Great

War for Empire" the bills of exchange served as a convenient means for provisioning English and American soldiers held prisoner by the French.[8] After the war the surveyor who fixed the boundary line between New York and Quebec was to be compensated in part by the Province of New York. One half of his fee was paid by a bill of exchange drawn upon Governor William Tryon. The bill was protested as the governor was not at home and had left no instructions for its payment; it would appear that it was subsequently paid since no pleadings are attached to the manuscript record of the transaction.[9]

Even before the American Revolution settlers began to cross the Appalachian mountain barrier and enter the fertile Ohio River Valley. With them they carried eastern business techniques, and the Anglo-American legal system. As early as 1770 the New York Court of Chancery heard a case arising from a bill of exchange executed in the "Illinois country."[10] A century of practice in New York, and other colonial seaports, formed the basis for extending the law of negotiable instruments to the interior of America. The province of New York had ceased to be a recipient of legal principles and was beginning to spread those rules in the back country of the vast American continent.

APPENDICES

The following chart is a graphic representation of figures reported by Sir Charles Whitworth concerning the trade of Great Britain with the Province of New York. As a member of Parliament from 1747 to 1778, Whitworth (1714-1778) had observed the rapid growth of the British Empire. He had served as chairman of the Ways and Means Committee from 1768 and would continue to so serve until his death in 1778. In 1755 he had been elected vice-president of the Society for the Encouragement of Arts, Manufactures and Commerce, and in the years prior to the publication of *The State of the Trade of Great Britain* he had authored many works on public finance and commercial activity.

£ thousands

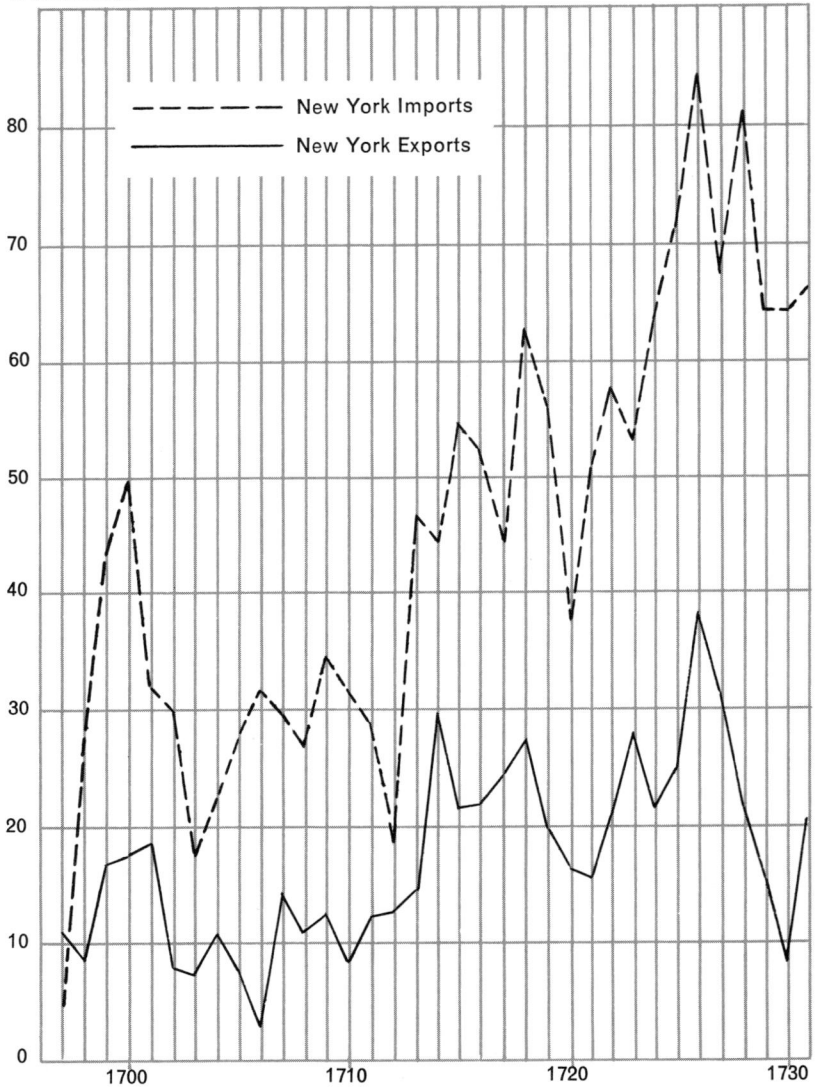

Commerce Between Great Britain and New York
1697-1730

The State of the Trade of Great Britain appeared in the fateful year of 1776 and was reprinted in French as *Commerce de la Grande-Bretagne* in the following year. The statistics in both editions are identical regarding the province of New York.

As customs officials made annual reports to the home government, these reports form the main basis for Whitworth's tables. Many of them were destroyed subsequent to 1776, or mere synopses of their contents remain. Thus the chart in Appendix B$_2$ of customs revenues is less complete than that produced here. It should also be noted that the factor of dishonest customs collection cannot be eliminated from any of these figures.

APPENDIX B$_1$

Population—New York

This chart is a graphic presentation of the details collected in Evarts B. Green and Virginia B. Harrington, *American Population Before the Federal Census of 1790*. In the course of my research I have had the opportunity to verify the statistics in Edmund B. O'Callaghan's *Documents Relative to the Colonial History of New York* and in the manuscript notes of George Chalmers. In both instances I found the data reported by Professor Green and Miss Harrington to be accurate.

The chart at best represents estimates arrived at from unofficial and rather informal surveys of the population. It was not until 1698 that there were any actual census figures and these, generally, were only partial.

Thousands

50

45

40

35

30

25

20

15

10

5

0

1670   1680   1690   1700   1710   1720   1730

(Dutch)

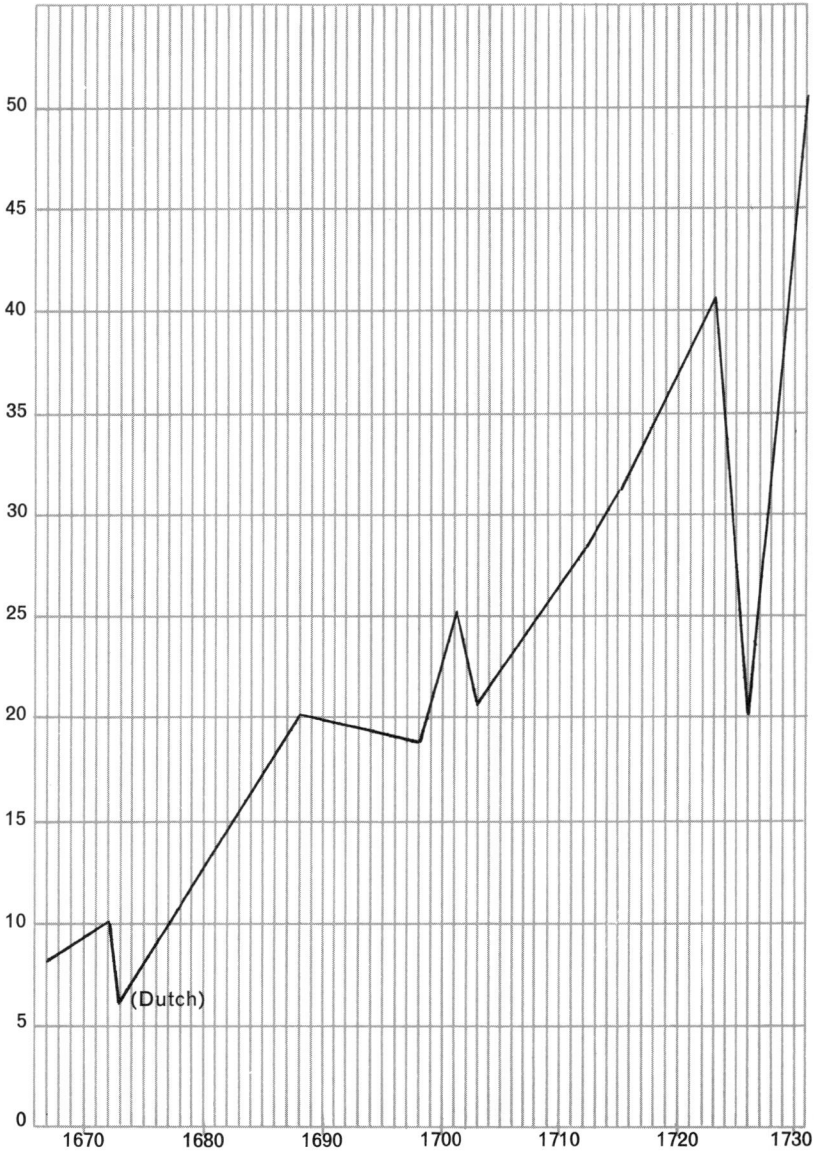

Population—New York

APPENDIX B₂

Customs Revenue—New York

Revenue figures for 1675-1677 are based on a custom inspector's estimate that revenues for the three years should total £14,000, or an average of £4,666 per year. The local merchants who provided information for the inspector inclined toward the figure of £5,600 per year. The likelihood is that actual collections amounted to about £4,000 per annum. In 1685 a total of £3,000 was collected for the year, but a governor's audit discovered a shortage of £3,000, raising the total revenue to £6,000.[1] George Chalmers reports £3,209.13.3¼ as customs revenue for 1687, but I have found no verification for this figure which Chalmers reports in great detail.[2] The figures reported for 1692 to 1697 by Chalmers are verified for 1692 to 1695 by Edmund B. O'Callaghan.[3] Their figures vary by a small amount which indicates a separate source of information. Figures for 1699 and 1700 are those stated by O'Callaghan, but not noted by Chalmers.[4] A verification for the customs figures from 1692 to 1696 appears in *Documents Relative to the Colonial History of New York*, Volume IV, page 173.

In the two-year period ending July 1, 1714, customs revenues totaled £3,222.1.6½ according to Chalmers, a figure for which I have not found verification nor contrary evidence.[5] The revenues reported for 1722 to 1725 are as given in O'Callaghan's *Documentary History*.[6]

£ thousands

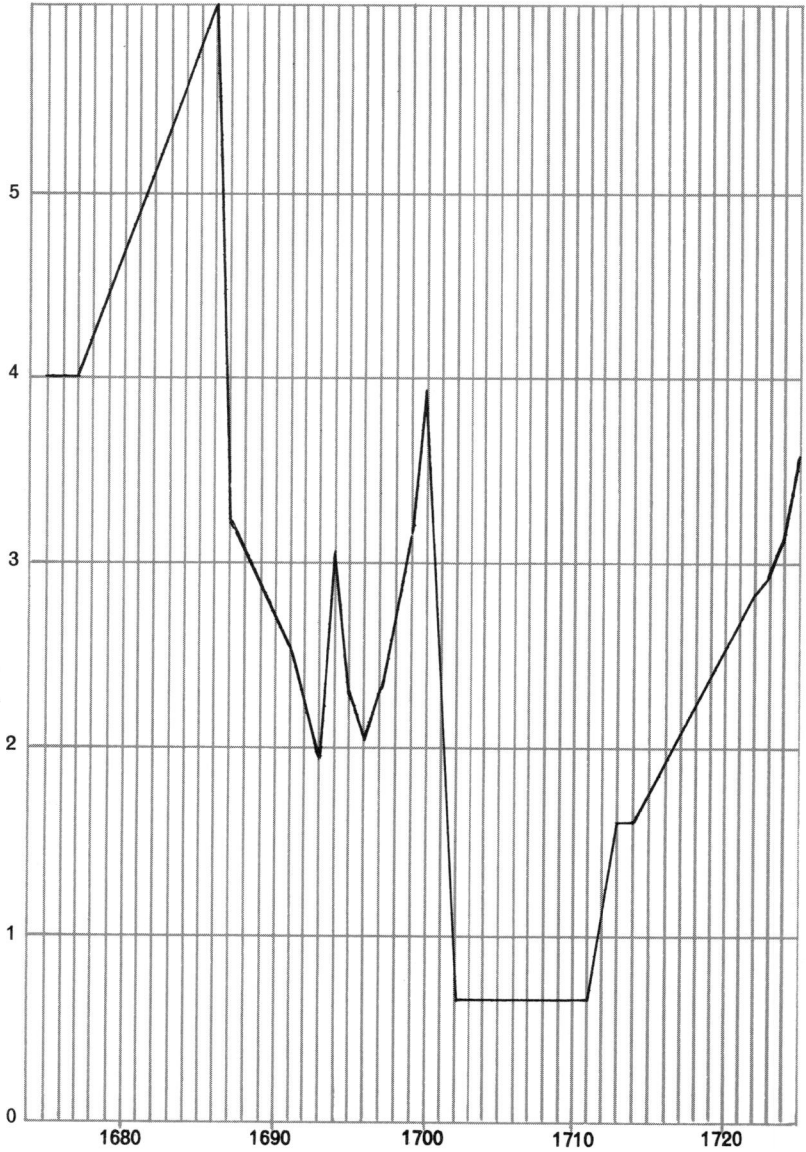

Customs Revenue—New York

APPENDIX C

Bills of Exchange

July 14

Worthy, right deservet Mr. Luyhas Arents, Greeting:

Whereas I am authorized by the late Shipper [first name illegible] Deught, as well as by letters of Cornelius van Delven-drip, notary at the Hague, to address myself to you, so I make bold to request you hereby to pay, eight days after sight of my bill of exchange dated 19 [*sic*] July 1662, to Shipper Jan Jansen Bestevaar or his order, on my account, the sum of Fifty guilders current money in cash I shall thankfully satisfy you. These then serving for advice, if I should not come to speak personally to you before this is handed to you, as I am about to sail in the Ship Arent.

Was signed TOBIAS FECKE[7]

Southampton, 12d Apr 1696

Mr. John Wick, please to pay unto Tho. Stephens Tenn pounds fifteen shillings and place the same to Account of

Sir, your Friend

JOHN REEVES

[*Endorsed on reverse*]

Southampton, the 15th Apr 96

Received of Mr. John Wick Ten pounds nine shillings and six pence upon the Account of Mr. John Reeves, I Say Received

THO. STEPHENS, JUNR.[8]

S. Hampton, March 31st, 1703

Sir:

At too Days Sight of this my second bill of Exchange and My first not being payd, please to pay unto Capt: Thomas Wenham or his Order the Full and Just sum of Eighty pounds nine Schillings six pence and place it at the account of,

Sir, Your Humble Servant at Concord

JOHN WICK

To Capt. John Theobald,
Mercht: in New York
[*Endorsed on reverse*]

The contents of this second bill of Exchange Received upon the first [day of July] as Witness my hand

ICHABOD COOPER[9]

S. Hampton, July 4th, 1704

Mr. Henry Loyd,

Sir, Please to let Mr. Lucas have what mony you have of mine in your hands, which will oblige me, Sir,

Your very humble servant,

MARG: SYLVESTER

Newport, the 4th November, 1707
For Mr. Henry Lloyd, merchant In Boston
[*Endorsed on reverse*]

Boston, the 11th November 1707

Received from Mr. Henry Lloyd one hundred and fourty pounds Eighteen shillings six pence half penny for the account of Madam Silvester.

AUGUSTUS LUCAS[10]

£140.18.6½

Amboy, Feby 20th, 1718

Sir:

Please pay to James Alexander four pounds money of New Jersey, for so much indebted by me to the said James and place it to account of

Your servant,

SAMUEL BIRNELL

To John Parker, Esq.

[*Endorsed on reverse*]

Received the Contents of the within bill.

JAS: ALEXANDER[11]

Mr. James Alexander

Pray pay the Bearer or Alexander Walker or Order on demand [illegible] and place the same to Account of

Your very humble Servant

WM. G. KEARNY

Perth Amboy, 16 Nov, 1722

Accepted JAS: ALEXANDER

Received payment of the contents of the above bill by me.

WILLIAM THOMSON[12]

Sir:

Please to pay to my Brother, James Leonard, four pounds new York money on account of taken up the Negro man and this my order shall be a sufficient Discharge for the Same, which is all from,

Your Vary Humble Servant,

THO: LEONARD

30 Sept., 1729

Accepted: JAS: ALEXANDER, ESQ., at New York City

[Endorsed on reverse]

Received the Contents by order of James Leonard, my husband.

CHARITY LEONARD[13]

3rd Exchange for £10 Sterl.

New York, March 25th, 1743

Sir:

Att twenty days sight of this my third bill of Exchange (my first and second of the same tenor not paid) pay to James Alexander of New York, or order, the sum of ten pounds sterling for one half years salary as schoolmaster to the venerable Society in the City of New York value received here of the said James, make good payment and place it to the account of, Sir,

Your humble servant

THOMAS NOXON

To Wm Tryon, Esq.

Treasurer, to the honourable

Society for the propogation of the Gospell

in foreign parts or to the Treasurer for the time being.

[Endorsed on reverse]

Pay to Messrs Panhurst Fuarez on order or to my use,

JAS: ALEXANDER[14]

Virginia, July 26th, 1755
Exchange for £30—.

At Sixty Days sight of this my Third Bill of Exchange my First and Second (of the same Tenor and Date) not paid, pay to Mr. Charles Stewart or Order, the Sum of thirty pounds Sterling (Value here received) at Time make payment, and place it to Account of

Your Humble Servant,
WILKIN RANDOLPH [15]

To Mr. Buchanan
Merchant in London

NOTES

CHAPTER I

1 Four obligations based on trade with the southern English colonies appear in the MS Register of Solomon LaChair, Notary Public of New Amsterdam 1661-1664, translated by Edmund B. O'Callaghan, Office of the New York City Clerk, pp. 2, 57, 184, 260-61. See also William I. Roberts, III, *The Fur Trade of New England in the Seventeenth Century*, p. 158 (Ann Arbor, Michigan: University Microfilms, 1958).

2 Berthold Fernow, editor, *The Records of New Amsterdam from 1653 to 1674 Anno Domini*, IV, pp. 15, 189, 255, 298, 309, 338. 7 vols. New York: Knickerbocker Press, 1897. Hereafter this work will be cited *R.N.A.*

3 In a case involving 21,265 pounds of Virginia tobacco, the planter offered to deliver in New England by means of an English vessel. The court ordered delivery in New Amsterdam in fourteen days (*ibid.*, p. 298). Similar cases appear in *ibid.*, pp. 300, 309 (1663).

4 A cargo of tobacco was discharged at Oyster Bay on Long Island in 1663, apparently to avoid the prohibitions of the Acts of Trade (*ibid.*, p. 189).

5 An official obtained an increase in fees because of this in November 1662 (*ibid.*, p. 188).

6 *Ibid.*, p. 153. Sewan was unstrung shell beads used in the fur trade with the Algonquian and Iroquois Indians. Its value arose from its equivalent in fur

pelts. Another factor which may have depressed the value of sewan could have been the epidemic illnesses which infected the Indians during the period 1658 to 1666. A scarcity of furs caused by illness of Indian hunters could have raised the price of furs and depressed the value of sewan. For discussion of epidemics see John Duffy, *Epidemics in Colonial America*, pp. 45, 223 (Baton Rouge: Louisiana State University Press, 1953) ; and David M. Ellis, James A. Frost, Harold C. Syrett and Harry J. Carman, *A Short History of New York State*, p. 16 (Ithaca: Cornell University Press, 1957).

7   *R.N.A.*, IV, p. 153.

8   Indian raids in the Esopus were noted in *ibid.*, pp. 275, 288 (July 2 and August 21, 1663). A later reference suggesting a conference for defense is found in *ibid.*, p. 318.

9   Raised to 24 stivers for an eight-pound wheat loaf on March 13, 1663, and to 26 stivers for the same loaf on April 17, 1663 (*ibid.*, p. 230).

10 For instances of trade with Barbados see *R.N.A.*, VI, pp. 246, 247, 392; trade with Jamaica appears in *R.N.A.*, VII, p. 11; and in MS Calendar of the Proceedings of the Court of Assizes, 1665-1672, New York Public Library, p. 42. (This typescript was prepared in 1907 for Orville B. Ackerly from the original manuscripts in the New York State Library, which were destroyed by fire in 1910.)

11 Litigation concerning whales appears in the New York City Mayor's Court on July 25, 1665 (*R.N.A.*, V, p. 282). The Duke's Laws of 1665 required notice of drift whales cast ashore to be given to the governor and council (*The Colonial Laws of New York from the Year 1664 to the Revolution*, I, p. 66 [5 vols. Albany, New York: James B. Lyon, State Printer, 1894]. Hereafter this work will be cited *Col. Laws N.Y.*). A case concerning rights to beached whales appears in the Court of Assizes in October 1667 (Proceedings of the Court of Assizes, 1665-1672, p. 16) ; another case in that court is noted in Victor Hugo Paltsits, editor, *Minutes of the Executive Council of the Province of New York; Administration of Francis Lovelace, 1668-1673*, II, p. 687 (2 vols. Albany: State of New York, 1910). Also see the act of the General Assembly mentioned as having been passed on May 10, 1699 (*Col. Laws N.Y.*, I, p. 409).

12 I. N. Phelps Stokes, compiler, *The Iconography of Manhattan Island*, I, p. 173. 6 vols. New York: Robert H. Dodd, 1915.

13 *R.N.A.*, VII, p. 18. However on October 31, 1673, it was noted that ships no longer came from Barbados because of the Dutch occupation of New York. The Maryland trade was of sufficient magnitude to warrant Jacob Leisler's maintaining a factor there to purchase tobacco (*ibid.*, p. 74).

14 Export was prohibited on May 9, 1670, by the governor and council. On petition by the merchants the prohibition was lifted in October 1672, but a maximum selling price was imposed. The prohibition was again ordered on April 29, 1673. See Paltsits, *Minutes of the Executive Council*, I, p. 137; II, p. 519; and *Col. Laws N.Y.*, I, p. 96.

15 It would seem that the shortage of wheat became so critical during the Dutch reoccupation that it was necessary to import wheat from neighboring colonies (*R.N.A.*, VII, p. 100 [June 19, 1674]).

16 A petition for seven years' free trade was granted by the king on October 23, 1667, but was revoked by order in council on November 18, 1668, due to opposition by English merchants (Edmund B. O'Callaghan, editor, *Documents Relative to the Colonial History of New York*, III, pp. 167, 177 [15 vols. Albany, New York: Weed, Parsons and Company, 1853]. Hereafter this work will be cited *Doc. Rel. Col. Hist. N.Y.*). Curtis P. Nettles notes that New York was a leader in trading with the Dutch island of Curacao at the turn of the 17th century, and that the Dutch West Indies islands were the chief source of heavy coinage in New York (Curtis P. Nettles, *The Money Supply of the American Colonies before 1720*, pp. 86, 87 [Madison: The University of Wisconsin Press, 1934]).

17 MS Minutes of the Mayor's Court, City of New York, November 13, 1674, to September 21, 1675, Office of the New York County Clerk, pp. 38, 61; Lawrence H. Leder and Vincent P. Carosso, "Robert Livingston (1654-1728): Businessman of Colonial New York," *Business History Review*, XXX (March 1956), p. 27.

18 For successive attempts to create uniform weights and measures of English origin see *Col. Laws N.Y.*, I, pp. 64 (in 1665), 95 (in 1672), 98 (in 1675); also the letter of Lord Cornbury to the Lords of the Treasury dated July 12, 1703, recommending confirmation of an act establishing English weights and measures (*Doc. Rel. Col. Hist. N.Y.*, IV, p. 1064). See act in *Col. Laws N.Y.*, I, p. 554.

19 Extensive commercial correspondence in Dutch is in MS Papers of Abraham DePeyster, 1695-1710, New-York Historical Society, fol. 60-91.

20 Gabriell Minviell to Sir John Werden, March 1685 (*Doc. Rel. Col. Hist. N.Y.*, III, p. 361).

21 *Ibid.*, pp. 362, 363.

22 *Ibid.*, p. 428.

23 For instances of Bostonian interest in New York trade see *R.N.A.*, VI, p. 315 (Bostonian admitted as burgher in 1671); and Leder and Carosso, "Robert Livingston," p. 22 (commercial relations with John Hull of Boston).

24 *Ibid.*, pp. 22, 27.

25 *Ibid.*, p. 27.

26 *Ibid., passim.*

27 Lord Cornbury to Lords of the Treasury, December 12, 1702 (*Doc. Rel. Col. Hist. N.Y.*, IV, p. 1017).

28 Privateer enterprise also extended to New York; see *Doc. Rel. Col. Hist. N.Y.*, III, p. 833 (Summer 1692); IV, p. 293 (November 1697).

29 Earl of Bellomont to Lords of the Treasury, May 25, 1698 (*ibid.*, p. 317).

30 While poverty seems to have been extreme in 1692, the situation seems to have improved thereafter. For 1692 see *Doc. Rel. Col. Hist. N.Y.*, III, pp. 813, 848, 854.

31 *Doc. Rel. Col. Hist. N.Y.*, IV, p. 932; Nettles, *Money Supply*, pp. 99-101, 107. Further indication of the primacy of Boston may be gained from the following average figures for English imports into North American colonies, derived from statistics reported in Sir Charles Whitworth, *State of the Trade of Great Britain in Its Imports and Exports*, pp. 63-66 (London: G. Robinson, J. Rob-

son, J. Walter, T. Cadell, J. Sewall, 1776).

Period	New York	New England	Pennsylvania
1697-1698	£14,929	£80,992	£6,851
1699-1708	£31,021	£86,006	£12,387
1709-1718	£44,535	£128,397	£14,755

32 Madagascar trade (*Doc. Rel. Col. Hist. N.Y.*, IV, pp. 304, 412, 446); there was also illegal trade in East India goods that had not made the required stop in England (*ibid.*, pp. 412, 475).

33 *Col. Laws N.Y.*, I, pp. 345, 346.

34 *Doc. Rel. Col. Hist. N.Y.*, IV, pp. 320, 416, 490, 604, 623.

35 Earl of Bellomont to Lords of the Treasury, December 14, 1698 (*ibid.*, p. 438).

36 *Ibid.*, pp. 781-97, 824, 855.

37 *Ibid.*, p. 848.

38 *Col. Laws N.Y.*, I, p. 637. By an act of the Assembly dated May 24, 1709, all provisions were removed from the export trade except wheat and bread, indicating that such surpluses occurred even in times of provision scarcity. In March of 1715, 370 bushels of winter wheat were shipped from New York to Boston ("Papers of the Lloyd Family of the Manor of Queens Village, Lloyd's Neck, Long Island, New York, 1654-1826" [Volume I, 1654-1752], in *Collections of the New-York Historical Society for the Year 1926*, LIX, p. 206 [New York: The Society, 1927]).

39 *Doc. Rel. Col. Hist. N.Y.*, V, pp. 57, 460, 686.

40 Lord Cornbury to Board of Trade, July 1, 1708 (*ibid.*, p. 57).

41 Lieutenant Governor Richard Ingoldesby to Lord Nottingham, June 14, 1704 (*Doc. Rel. Col. Hist. N.Y.*, IV, p. 1090).

42 *A Dialogue Between a Member of Parliament, a Divine, a Lawyer, a Freeholder, a Shopkeeper and a Country Farmer*, pp. 2-4. Anonymous pamphlet published in England in 1703, Columbia University Special Collections Library.

43 *Doc. Rel. Col. Hist. N.Y.*, V, p. 686. Nettles indicates that prosperity in the colonies during the years 1710-1713 was due to the English bills of exchange which were drawn to cover military expenditures (Nettles, *Money Supply*, p. 94). Very likely a combination of the two factors gave New York her "good times" during the last years of Queen Anne's War.

44 MS Notes of George Chalmers, New York Public Library, I, p. 30.

45 *Doc. Rel. Col. Hist. N.Y.*, V, p. 460 (November 1715).

46 *Ibid.*, pp. 497 (January 1718), 686 (1723). See also the anonymous, MS Trade of the Port of New York (Colony), 1711, p. 10 (photostat), New York Public Library.

47 *Doc. Rel. Col. Hist. N.Y.*, V, p. 601 (1721); Carl Bridenbaugh, *Cities in the Wilderness; the First Century of Urban Life in America, 1625-1742*, p. 332 (New York: Ronald Press, 1938).

48 Bill of lading, June 10, 1703 (Abraham DePeyster Papers, fol. 85).

49 Bill of lading, January 2, 1703 (*ibid.*, fol. 71).

50 Bill of lading, August 24, 1702 (*ibid.*, fol. 59); *Doc. Rel. Col. Hist. N.Y.*, V, p. 379 (1714, rum an important part of excises).

51　Lloyd Family Papers, p. 188.

52　*Doc. Rel. Col. Hist. N.Y.*, V, p. 300 (1712).

53　An instance of a New York merchant being outbid on freight rates to England appears in the Abraham DePeyster Papers, fol. 25.

54　MS Papers of John Wick of Northampton, Long Island, New York, Wick-Blachly-Colles Papers, Correspondence and Papers, 1688-1925, Box labeled Correspondence 1688-1745, New York Public Library. Also in the collection see bills of lading dated June 12, 1714, and February 1714, and the letter of William Donne of Bristol dated March 30, 1715.

55　"Letters and Papers of Cadwallader Colden" (Volume I, 1711-1729), in *Collections of the New-York Historical Society for the Year 1917*, L, pp. 42, 43 (New York: The Society, 1918). While the New England merchants were able to trade directly with England, the New York merchants usually dealt with agents of London merchants resident in New York (Nettles, *Money Supply*, pp. 73, 74).

56　See Appendix A for a graphic illustration of New York's trade deficit during the years 1697 to 1730. It would seem that the shortage became critical during the years 1713-1730 (Lloyd Family Papers, pp. 203-05, 241), and the calling in of bills of credit seems to have aggravated the already bad situation (*ibid.*, p. 223). See also *Doc. Rel. Col. Hist. N.Y.*, V, p. 462; Nettles, *Money Supply*, p. 85.

57　For New York Assembly action concerning foreign coin and its valuation see *Col. Laws N.Y.*, I, pp. 97, 521, 678. Discovery of copper ores caused suggestions that it might serve as money (*Doc. Rel. Col. Hist. N.Y.*, V, p. 461; "Letters and Papers of Cadwallader Colden" [Volume VIII, Additional Letters and Papers, 1715-1748], in *Collections of the New-York Historical Society for the Year 1934*, LXVIII, p. 71 [New York: The Society, 1937]).

58　The price of silver in Massachusetts provincial bills rose from nine shillings, two pence per ounce in 1716 to sixteen shillings per ounce in 1727. In other words the bills declined to half of their 1716 value within a period of eleven years ("Letters and Papers of Cadwallader Colden," I, pp. 244-46). See also Lloyd Family Papers, p. 267.

59　New York bills were in greater demand than were the bills of Pennsylvania in the city of Philadelphia ("Letters and Papers of Cadwallader Colden," I, pp. 57, 58 [1724]) and they sold at a premium over the bills of Massachusetts at the Exchange in Boston (*Doc. Rel. Col. Hist. N.Y.*, V, p. 494). In the face of a 500 percent increase in the number of New York bills outstanding in 1720 (£36,000) over those outstanding in 1710 (£7,000), the discount on New York bills in relation to English currency rose from 33⅓ percent in 1710 to 70 percent in 1720. For New York bills outstanding see *A Statistical Abstract Supplement: Historical Statistics of the United States, Colonial Times to 1957*, p. 774 (Washington: U.S. Department of Commerce, 1960). For value of New York bills in English currency see *Doc. Rel. Col. Hist. N.Y.*, V, p. 170 (1710) and "Letters and Papers of Cadwallader Colden," I, p. 47 (1720). Nettles notes that depreciation of bills of credit set in after 1713, but does not compare the relative value of New York and Massachusetts bills (Nettles, *Money Supply*, Chapter 10).

60 The act, reprinted in *Col. Laws N.Y.*, I, p. 909, is essentially the same as the English statute 12 Car. II, c. 13 (1660), which was considered by colonial lawyers to apply to New York; see a defense of usurious interest interposed in the case of Stephens v. Van Hooke (1693), in MS Mayor's Court Papers, Benjamin Salzer Collection, Box 1, Columbia University Special Collections Library. It would, therefore, appear that the action of the General Assembly was merely a declaration of the preexisting law of the province. In 1718 the Assembly raised the legal interest rate to 8 percent, and the rate remained at that level until 1738, at which time it was reduced to 7 percent (*Col. Laws N.Y.*, I, pp. 1004, 1005; II, pp. 980, 981). As far as can be determined the acts were never considered by the Privy Council, and were not annulled as repugnant to the law of England.

61 For population growth see Appendix B_1, for trade with Great Britain see Appendix A. During the years 1727-1730 outward shipping generally declined 2 percent, but exports to Great Britain decreased 80 percent. Inward activity decreased by about 1.6 percent, while imports from Great Britain decreased 8.1 percent. Figures for general port activity from *A Statistical Abstract Supplement*, p. 774.

62 By the act of October 29, 1730, the General Assembly set up a system for judicial proceedings in the nature of bankruptcy, thereby giving us additional evidence of the extent of the depression (*Col. Laws N.Y.*, II, pp. 669-75).

CHAPTER II

1 Some indication of the highly developed Dutch civil law that was applied in New Amsterdam may be had by considering the list of Dutch law texts in the possession of the Court of Burgomasters, Schepens, and Schout in 1674 (*R.N.A.*, VII, p. 139). The collection included texts on Dutch admiralty law, practice, bylaws of Amsterdam, and the ordinances of the States General. See also the pleading of Solomon LaChair citing six legal texts, including Hugo Grotius's *Introduction to the Jurisprudence of Holland* (Register of Solomon LaChair, p. 385).

2 Written in 1620 as a book of instructions for his sons, the work was first published in 1631 and immediately became a classic exposition of Dutch law. Its significance was enhanced by its being the first legal treatise to be published in Dutch rather than Latin (Hugo Grotius, *The Jurisprudence of Holland*, translated by Robert Warden Lee, I, pp. vii, xii [2 vols. Oxford: Clarendon Press, 1926]).

3 Alexander N. Sack, *Conflicts of Laws in the History of English Law*, p. 344 (New York: New York University Press, 1937), cites a case decided as late as 1683 where the inheritance laws peculiar to London were held applicable to a London merchant who died while traveling in the outlying counties.

4 Dutch civil law experienced no difficulty in absorbing the law merchant into its fabric. Its philosophic basis in natural law and its ready acceptance of changes made in the law by the practices of the people made it much more receptive to change than the common-law system.

5 Sack, *Conflicts of Laws*, p. 349.

6   William S. Holdsworth, *A History of English Law*, I, p. 542 (3rd ed. rev. 13 vols. London: Methuen and Company, 1922); Sack, *Conflicts of Laws*, p. 351. The statute conferring these privileges is 27 Edw. III, St. 2, c. 2 (1352), commonly called the Statute of the Staple.

7   Sack, *Conflicts of Laws*, pp. 352, 353, citing Fitzherbert, *New Natura Brevium*, p. 114 (1534, 9th ed.; 1794).

8   "Munimenta Gildhallae Londoniensis: Liber Albus, Liber Custumarum, et Liber Horn," edited and translated by Henry Thomas Riley, in *Rerum Britannicarum Medii Aevi Scriptores, or Chronicles and Memorials of Great Britain and Ireland During the Middle Ages*, XII, Part III, p. 115 (London: Longmans, Brown, Green, Longmans and Roberts, 1859-1862). This particular section is commonly referred to as *Liber Albus* and, according to the editor, the White Book of London was compiled in 1419 by John Carpenter, then the town clerk of London.

9   Alice Beardwood, *Alien Merchants in England 1350 to 1377, Their Legal and Economic Position*, pp. 24, 39 (Cambridge, Massachusetts: Medieval Academy of America, 1931), indicates that the foreign merchants served as financial agents of the kingdom, moneylenders, and trading agents; in return for this they were required to pay higher customs to the Exchequer than did English merchants.

10   Sack, *Conflicts of Laws*, p. 351, citing 17 Edw. IV, c. 2 (1477) and the perpetuating statute 1 Rich. III, c. 6 (1483).

11   *Ibid.*, p. 314.

12   *Liber Custumarum (Rerum Britannicarum Medii Aevi Scriptores)*, Part II (2), p. xciv, gives an excellent indication of England's economic dependence on the continent in the fifteenth century.

13   The last Venetian galley left the Thames in 1532 (Charles M. Andrews, *The Colonial Period of American History*, I, p. 27 [4 vols. New Haven: Yale University Press, 1934]).

14   *Ibid.*, p. 28. The Steelyard was a sizable plot of land on the London waterfront which was occupied by the representatives of the Hanse League in London. Under the peculiar legal arrangement, the merchants were subject to the rules of the league and not to the laws of England. Their status was not unlike that enjoyed by American residents in China during the period of operation of the consular courts.

15   Holdsworth, *History of English Law*, I, p. 526.

16   J. Milnes Holden, *The History of Negotiable Instruments in English Law*, p. 19 (London: Athlone Press, 1955). Unlike procedure at common law, it was possible to arrest the defendant or to attach his property prior to his defiance of a writ issued to commence the suit. After the judgment was rendered for the complainant, the property could be sold to satisfy the judgment or the defendant imprisoned until the judgment was satisfied.

17   *Ibid.*, p. 418, n. 147.

18   Holdsworth, *History of English Law*, I, p. 552; Sack, *Conflicts of Laws*, p. 354.

19   *Ibid.*, p. 358. It would seem that this development antedated the growth of the jurisdiction of the Court of Admiralty into civil causes.

20 *Ibid.*, p. 345. The reason for the opposition of the higher house is not given, but it may have been to stem the growing power of the monarchy and the commercial classes. As a landed class the peers probably saw no need for such a radical alteration in the powers of the common-law courts.

21 In the pleading the litigant alleged that the events giving rise to the cause of action arose at a specified foreign place, which, he alleged, was located in the ward of the city or the county of England in which the court heard the case. This pleading was not subject to refutation by the defending party, and thus conferred the necessary venue on the action and gave the court jurisdiction. Such pleadings were used in both the Mayor's Court of London and the New York City Mayor's Court.

22 Henry Campbell Black, *Law Dictionary*, p. 1727. 4th ed. St. Paul, Minnesota: West Publishing Company, 1951.

23 In cases involving the title to real property arising out of adverse possession, and in criminal causes, the venue system still retains its ancient rationale and validity.

24 *Liber Albus (Rerum Britannicarum Medii Aevi Scriptores)*, Part III, pp. 43, 44.

25 *Ibid.*, pp. 51, 247.

26 *Ibid.*, p. 50.

27 Sack, *Conflicts of Laws*, pp. 343-45. To be specific, the English courts would accept proof of foreign law if such proof were material to facts in issue, but the rights and liabilities of the parties would be determined in regard to English legal principles, and not those principles which prevailed at the place of the act which formed the basis of the suit.

28 Albert Venn Dicey, *Conflict of Laws*, edited by J. H. C. Morris, p. 5 (6th ed. London: Stevens and Sons, 1949), places the origin of the conflicts system in the nineteenth century. Joseph Story, *Commentaries on the Conflicts of Laws*, edited by Melville M. Bigelow, p. 10 (8th ed. Boston: Little, Brown and Company, 1883), places the growth of the conflicts theory in the eighteenth century. Mr. Justice Story's experience with maritime law may be the reason for his more accurate estimate.

29 Holdsworth, *History of English Law*, I, p. 570. One example of earlier reception of merchant customs is the "God's penny," a small sum of money to create a binding obligation; see 31 Edw. I (1303); *Liber Custumarum (Rerum Britannicarum Medii Aevi Scriptores)*, Part II (2), p. xxvi; Holdsworth, *History of English Law*, I, p. 569.

CHAPTER III

1 Based on the traditional Dutch community court of the same name, this court consisted of one schout (performed duties of sheriff and prosecuting attorney), two burgomasters (administrative officers of the city), and five schepens (aldermen and justices). Unlike its Dutch counterpart, the New Amsterdam court could not boast popular election of its members, who were appointed by the director general from a list of nominees submitted by the court (Richard B. Morris, editor, *Select Cases of the Mayor's Court of New*

York City 1674-1784, p. 41 [Washington: American Historical Association, 1935]).

2   *Ibid.*, p. 42.

3   Register of Solomon LaChair, p. 239. A pleading in which LaChair refers to customs of the city of Amsterdam as being in force in New Amsterdam.

4   On November 1, 1664, the court heard four parties in four separate suits justify their default in pleading or appearance on the identical ground—an injured foot and leg (*R.N.A.*, V, p. 149). The English eventually limited the litigants to one default before a nonsuit (*R.N.A.*, VI, p. 376 [1672]).

5   They were Adrian van de Donck, Dorck van Schalleyne, David Borvoost, Johannes de Decker, Matthias de Vos, Walewyn van der Veen, Tielman van Vleck, Pelgrum Clocq, and Solomon LaChair. LaChair was commissioned on January 20, 1661, but seems to have died in January of 1663. See Register of Solomon LaChair, p. 1; *R.N.A.*, IV, p. 175.

6   "Proceedings of the General Court of Assizes Held in the City of New York, October 6, 1680, to October 6, 1682," in *Collections of the New-York Historical Society for the Year 1912*, XLV, pp. 1-38 (New York: The Society, 1913). For provision in the Duke's Laws see *Col. Laws N.Y.*, I, p. 16.

7   The name of the court was changed on June 12, 1665, and the members took their new oaths of office on June 16 (*R.N.A.*, V, pp. 249-51). Professor Morris indicates that a change in the powers of the court was intended, but except for the introduction of the jury, no changes were made (Morris, *Select Cases of the Mayor's Court*, p. 45).

8   Paul M. Hamlin and Charles E. Baker, editors, *Supreme Court of Judicature of the Province of New York 1691-1704*, I, pp. 13-22 (3 vols. New York: New-York Historical Society, 1959). The act of the Assembly appears in *Col. Laws N.Y.*, I, p. 228.

9   As early as August 8, 1666, a suit for the detention of money decided for plaintiff on a jury verdict was allowed by the Mayor's Court to be appealed to the Court of Assizes, DeLavall v. Malby (*R.N.A.*, VI, p. 33). The court found it necessary to reverse judgments given by the Courts of Sessions at Gravesend and Jamaica in cases based upon negotiable instruments ("Proceedings of the General Court of Assizes," pp. 5, 6). It reversed a Mayor's Court judgment for £100, and granted leave to appeal to the king in council, Hall v. Darvall (*ibid.*, p. 7). Apparently the Court of Assizes could reverse on both the law and the facts (*ibid.*, p. 32). An example of removal of a cause to the Court of Oyer and Terminer by habeas corpus is Smith v. Corby (Mayor's Court Minutes, p. 136 [October 24, 1682-April 9, 1695]).

10 Hamlin and Baker, *Supreme Court of Judicature*, I, pp. 67, 71. The act establishing the court appears in *Col. Laws N.Y.*, I, p. 228.

11 Nisi prius courts heard controversies and determined issues through one presiding judge and a jury. The court en banc heard appeals from nisi prius judgments as well as appeals from other inferior courts. For the hardship of circuit riding see Hamlin and Baker, *Supreme Court of Judicature*, I, p. 312. Salaries were moderate, the chief justice received £130 including the circuit allowance, and the second justice received £100 including the circuit allowance (*Doc. Rel. Col. Hist. N.Y.*, IV, p. 25 [1693]).

12 *Col. Laws N.Y.*, I, p. 228.
13 That few cases were appealed from Mayor's Court, see Morris, *Select Cases of the Mayor's Court*, p. 47.
14 On August 22, 1665, Governor Richard Nicolls created five commissioners of the Court of Admiralty, Captains Robert Needham, Thomas Willet, Thomas Topping, and Mr. Matthias Nicolls and Mr. John Laurence (MS Extracts on the Court of Assizes 1665-1672, Joseph W. Moulton Manuscript, New-York Historical Society). Of these commissioners Nicolls was the only English-trained lawyer, but John Laurence had received considerable legal training in his activities as a merchant (Hamlin and Baker, *Supreme Court of Judicature*, III, pp. 148, 122 ff.).
15 Judge Hough notes that there is no evidence of any writ of prohibition issuing out of the Supreme Court of Judicature to the Vice-admiralty Court, and believes that the restrictions on the admiralty jurisdiction were unknown in the province (Charles Merrill Hough, *Reports of Cases in the Vice Admiralty of the Province of New York and in the Court of Admiralty of the State of New York, 1715-1788*, pp. xix, xiii, xviii [New Haven: Yale University Press, 1925]). A consideration of the MS Abridgment by Roger Mompesson, Columbia University Law Library, p. 64, and its detailed consideration of the restrictions on the High Court of Admiralty, will leave little doubt that Judge Hough was misled by the lack of conflict over a point which the lawyers and judges of the province considered well settled. For an example of a prohibition issued by the governor and council against a suit pending in the New York Vice-admiralty Court, see the material on Archibald Kennedy *qui tam* v. The Mary and Margaret and Thomas Fowles, MS Papers of James Alexander, New-York Historical Society, Box 45; and *Doc. Rel. Col. Hist. N.Y.*, VI, pp. 154-55.
16 Hamlin and Baker, *Supreme Court of Judicature*, I, p. 4.
17 Hough, *Reports of Cases in the Vice Admiralty, passim*.
18 The act was passed November 11, 1692, and was confirmed by the Privy Council on May 11, 1697. It provided that governor and rulers of fairs were to be appointed by the governor, and to hold a "court of Pypowder with all the Libertyes and free Customs to such appertaining" (*Col. Laws N.Y.*, I, p. 298).
19 Fair courts at Stourbridge, Winchester, Boston, and Beverly survived to the eighteenth century (Morris, *Select Cases of the Mayor's Court*, pp. 3-4).
20 The records from 1653 to 1674 are printed in English in *R.N.A.*; a valuable selection of cases is printed in Morris, *Select Cases of the Mayor's Court*, which covers the period from 1674 to 1784. Manuscript collections cover all years subsequent to 1674 in their entirety, but the bulk of these records makes future publication unlikely.
21 *Ibid.*, p. 45; Hamlin and Baker, *Supreme Court of Judicature*, I, p. 144.
22 The indictment is in "Proceedings of the General Court of Assizes," p. 13.
23 See Morris, *Select Cases of the Mayor's Court*, p. 47; also *Col. Laws N.Y.*, I, p. 189.
24 Imposition of the minimum amount of forty shillings ordered by court on October 12, 1672 (*R.N.A.*, VI, pp. 393, 394). That this was the amount dur-

ing the period see MS John Chambers, Common Place Book (1703-1734), Columbia University Law Library, p. 210.

25   In Cousseau v. Van Tright, *R.N.A.*, VI, p. 209.

26   In the early proceedings the following are referred to as attorneys: Richard Morris (*ibid.*, pp. 331, 363) ; Jonathan Sharp (*ibid.*, p. 346; Proceedings of the Court of Assizes, 1665-1672, p. 7) ; John Rider and Anthony Waters (*ibid.*, p. 9). Throughout the period Matthias Nicolls appears as an attorney; he and Richard Morris seem to be the only members of the Inns of Court.

27   See Mayor's Court Minutes, October 24, 1682, to April 9, 1695, pp. 233 ff. (1694).

28   Of the attorneys practicing in 1691 only Matthias Nicolls, George Farewell, and Thomas Johnson were members of the Inns of Court, and the ablest members of the bar were without this formal training (Hamlin and Baker, *Supreme Court of Judicature*, I, pp. 83, 84). The nonmembers included James Emott, William Nicolls, Edward Antill, John Tudor, David Jamison, and James Graham (Paul M. Hamlin, "New York's First Bar Association," *New York Law Forum*, V [October 1959], pp. 352-53) ; see brief biographical sketches of these men in Hamlin and Baker, *Supreme Court of Judicature*, III. A total of fourteen lawyers arrived in the province in 1698 and 1701, of whom ten were members of the Inns of Court (Hamlin, "New York's First Bar Association," p. 354). Before this influx of new lawyers the members of the bar were so limited in number that a law was passed to prevent any person from retaining all of the available counsel to the detriment of his opponents (*Col. Laws N.Y.*, I, p. 351 [1695]). Among the arrivals after 1698 were Samuel Shelton Broughton and Roger Mompesson, both of whom were exceptionally well-qualified members of the Inns of Court (Hamlin and Baker, *Supreme Court of Judicature*, III, pp. 39, 130). See Roger Mompesson's exhaustive Abridgment.

29   Hamlin, "New York's First Bar Association," p. 362.

30   Morris, *Select Cases of the Mayor's Court*, p. 53; one of the lawyers so benefited copied the information in his notebook (Chambers, Common Place Book, p. 209).

31   Nonsuit because of variance between writ and declaration (Mayor's Court Minutes, October 24, 1682, to April 9, 1695, p. 130) is an early example of this type of formalism (1684).

32   For foreign merchant custom see *R.N.A.*, VI, p. 186; for venue pleadings, Mayor's Court Minutes, August 20, 1723, to April 30, 1728, p. 443.

33   Promissory notes seem the result of the English statute of 1704. As instruments of credit their use is of necessity based upon the loan of funds. Since New York had but little excess currency there was little need for notes in addition to the formal obligation. There was even less need that the notes should be assignable.

CHAPTER IV

1 The motto, somewhat paradoxically, is the slogan of the largest credit reference concern in the United States, Dun and Bradstreet, Inc.

2 In Dutch law, the informal writing gave a preference to the assets in the
   debtor's estate only if it was executed before three witnesses (Grotius, *Jurisprudence of Holland*, I, p. 333). An example of an early form of English
   note appears in the Register of Solomon LaChair, pp. 17, 19. Throughout the
   years 1661-1664 the Dutch at New Amsterdam used the terms "note" and
   "obligation" interchangeably, but the terms of these notes indicate that they
   were not obligations.

3 Register of Solomon LaChair. In some instances the obligation was executed
   before the secretary of the province because the security was real estate, and
   rights to land were transferable only by the secretary (*ibid.*, p. 400; but see
   also p. 272 where this procedure was not followed). Another mention of an
   obligation executed before the secretary is *R.N.A.*, IV, p. 67. See also Grotius,
   Jurisprudence of Holland, I, p. 333.

4 Register of Solomon LaChair; MS Register of Walewyn van der Veen,
   Notary Public of New Amsterdam, 1662-1664, translated by Edmund B.
   O'Callaghan, Office of the New York City Clerk. A signature by mark ap-
   pears in the Register of Solomon LaChair, p. 40.

5 *Ibid.*

6 *Ibid.*, pp. 299, 71. In the latter case the wife held a power of attorney from
   her husband.

7 DeMayer v. Symondsen, *R.N.A.*, IV, p. 306 (1663).

8 An assignee of an obligation was precluded from proceeding against the
   obligor's real property because the original creditor had not received a property interest in the realty by having the obligation executed before the secretary of the province (*ibid.*, p. 321). At the same time, however, the narratives
   in the obligations include recitations of preexisting debts which bear no relationship to the transaction giving rise to the obligation (Register of Solomon LaChair, p. 315).

9 *Ibid.*, *passim*; Register of Walewyn van der Veen.

10 LaChair's fees seem to have increased as his practice grew. He charged two
   florins, ten stivers for an obligation in English in November 1661. In 1662 he
   charged three florins, ten stivers as a fee for drawing an obligation (Register
   of Solomon LaChair, pp. 298, 368). An example of an obligation drawn but
   not executed appears at *ibid.*, p. 109.

11 A note burned because of carelessness was rewritten for an additional fee
   (*ibid.*, p. 300).

12 An obligation, later the subject of a lawsuit, was conveyed before LaChair
   and two witnesses on October 13, 1661 (*R.N.A.*, IV, p. 10). LaChair did not
   record this transaction in his register, and we have no similar conveyance
   available in either of the notarial registers cited.

13 A conveyance of a part interest in an obligation is noted in the Register of
   Solomon LaChair, p. 57. The original obligation was kept by the creditor,
   while a duplicate with the transfer noted was forwarded to the assignee.

14 The inability of an assignee to proceed against the property of the obligor because of the error of the assignor has been discussed on page 68, note 8. In Steenwyck v. Anthony (*R.N.A.*, IV, p. 105), the plaintiff was ordered to obtain settlement of accounts between his assignor, who was in Holland, and the defendant, before attempting to proceed further with his suit on the defendant's obligation.

15 In the Register of Solomon LaChair, pp. 260, 261, there are two "notes" which are in the form of obligations. On the back there is noted, "Mr. Sam Smith, please pay the within to Frederick Gysberts and this shall be for you a discharge." The direction, in the form of a contemporary bill of exchange, seems to be merely the appointment of an agent for collection. For an unsuccessful attempt to proceed on the basis of an oral authorization of a man believed by the court to be deceased, see *R.N.A.*, IV, p. 120.

16 Grotius, *Jurisprudence of Holland*, I, p. 331; *R.N.A.*, V, p. 52.

17 See Croesens v. Hollingwoort [Hollingworth], *R.N.A.*, IV, p. 81; for a case where the defendant denied receipt of a certificate of notice and protest see Rasenbergh v. Stein, *R.N.A.*, V, p. 65.

18 A plaintiff appeared in court and requested the court's permission to garnish an indebtedness owed by a third party to the defendant. As the debt was evidenced by an obligation, the court refused to permit the garnishment unless the obligation was presented in open court. Since the obligation was physically located in Holland, the plaintiff's suit to garnish the debt was eventually dismissed (*R.N.A.*, IV, p. 113). The court would order the obligation returned to obligor upon full payment of the principal sum and any interest accrued (*ibid.*, p. 287; V, p. 65).

19 Grotius, *Jurisprudence of Holland*, I, p. 331.

20 *R.N.A.*, IV, pp. 69, 118, 205.

21 *R.N.A.*, VI, p. 275 (1671). See the discussion of interest on page 62, note 60.

22 The provision in the Duke's Laws appears in *Col. Laws N.Y.*, I, p. 17. It specifically makes bills and specialties assignable. By bill it seems safe to assume that the intention was to include a bill obligatory, that is, an obligation that had been formally executed, but not to include an informal obligation executed without witness or seal or notarial act.

23 As to obligation see William Sheppard, *A Grand Abridgment of the Common and Statute Law of England*, I, p. 476 (2 vols. London: E. Flesher, J. Streater, and H. Twyford, 1675). As to informal note see Holden, *History of Negotiable Instruments*, pp. 66-75.

24 *R.N.A.*, V, p. 125 (1664); VI, pp. 19 (1666), 165 (1669).

25 *Ibid.*, pp. 121, 169, 360. For assignability see *ibid.*, p. 383 (1672).

26 The penal bill seems to have taken its inspiration from the recognizance used to secure a party's presence at court. The penal bill provided that a certain sum was to be paid at a certain time, and if it were, the bill would be void. However the bill expressed the amount due as twice that which was to be paid on the due date, giving the creditor a 100 percent increase on his money in the event the borrower defaulted. It is possible that the bond mentioned in *ibid.*, p. 275, is of this nature.

27 See discussion on pages 30-31.

28 "Proceedings of the General Court of Assizes," p. 32 (1680). A personal defense to an instrument is a claim for avoidance of the instrument, based upon a legal defect in the transaction which produced the instrument. On the other hand, fraud in the inducement to execute the instrument is what is termed a real defense.

29 Roger Mompesson's Abridgment, p. 88. From the extensive citation of precedents it must be assumed that Mompesson prepared the volume while he resided in England. Such an extensive collection of English reports and texts could not have been found in America.

30 Some examples of suits on penal bills obligatory are in "Minutes of the Supreme Court of Judicature, April 4, 1693, to April 1, 1701," in *Collections of the New-York Historical Society for the Year 1912*, XLV, p. 132 (New York: The Society, 1913); Mayor's Court Minutes, November 13, 1674, to September 21, 1675, p. 2. See discussion on page 62, note 60, concerning the operation of the usury statute in the province of New York. For specific allegation of English statute as defense to penal bill, see Mayor's Court Papers, Box 1 (1693). For recovery of more than the amount advanced against English law in 1719, see "Letters and Papers of Cadwallader Colden," VIII, p. 49.

31 Mayor's Court Minutes.

32 The act appears in *Col. Laws N.Y.*, II, p. 676; it is noteworthy that it was enacted on the same day as the bankruptcy statute mentioned on page 62, note 62.

33 The act is entitled, "A Bill Concerning the Assignment of Specialtyes," and appears in *Col. Laws N.Y.*, I, p. 153.

34 The Dutch practice of conveying a formal obligation is discussed on pages 29-30, and the appointment of a collecting agent is also discussed there.

35 This seems a return in principle to the Dutch practice, for in English law only recognizances were recorded in court records. However the Dutch system of conveying an obligation before a notary public was probably more expeditious and inexpensive.

36 It seems safe to assume that the Assembly meant informal obligations to be included in the term "notes in writing." The goldsmith's notes had been in use in England since about 1680 (Holden, *History of Negotiable Instruments*, pp. 70-72), and it is likely that the term had gained the technical meaning, that is, that of an informal bill obligatory.

37 Rediscount is the process whereby a creditor sells his interest to a third party, usually at slightly less than the principal amount of the debt. It is particularly helpful to those who cannot afford to hold any part of their assets in accounts or notes receivable. Rediscount of open accounts is termed factoring.

38 An interesting discussion of this limiting date is in Hamlin and Baker, *Supreme Court of Judicature*, I, pp. 379-81.

39 It should be recalled that the Mayor's Court had jurisdiction of all suits of forty shillings or more. With the decline in value of provincial currency, this was not a particularly large amount, and it would seem that if any informal

bills obligatory were used at least a few would have become the subject of a lawsuit.

40   The statute is 3, 4 Annae, c. 8 (1704) ; although it is popularly known as the Promissory Note Act it refers only to "notes in writing."

41   Mayor's Court Papers, Box 2.

42   Morris, *Select Cases of the Mayor's Court*, p. 513 (1729).

43   MS Note Book of Joseph Murray, Columbia University Law Library, p. 137; a narrative of an assignee of a promissory note against the drawer.

44   See Churchill v. Hood, Mayor's Court Minutes, September 26, 1704, to November 21, 1710, p. 509 (June 27, 1710), where a note of £6.7.6 was assigned by endorsement to the plaintiff.

45   For mention of merchant customs, see *ibid.*, May 6, 1718, to June 14, 1720, p. 5 (1718) ; for mention of commerce between parties, see the foregoing and also p. 112 in the same volume (1718). While the allegation of the statute remains to the end of the period, the allegations of having commerce and of parties being subject to the customs of the merchants disappear about 1720; see *ibid.*, August 20, 1723, to April 30, 1728, pp. 197, 232 (1725).

46   Assumpsit is an action based upon the tortious acquisition of the property of another by the use of fraud and deceit. It was extremely popular at this time, and the minutes of the Mayor's Court are full of allegations in assumpsit. The prime disadvantage to suing in assumpsit rather than on the note would be the higher fee charged by the attorney for drawing the lengthy plea in assumpsit. If the holder of a promissory note wished to recover damages for failure to pay on the due date, he declared in assumpsit. A jury was assembled to fix his damages. In the case of a writing obligatory, the court fixed the damages without summoning a jury.

47   Morris, *Select Cases of the Mayor's Court*, p. 513; Mayor's Court Minutes, May 6, 1718, to June 14, 1720, p. 5.

48   The change involved the statute of limitations covering suits on notes under seal. Prior to 1941 a twenty-year statute of limitations applied alike to suits upon judgments and suits upon sealed instruments. By laws of 1941, Chapter 329, Sections 2 and 6, the presence of a seal was declared to be of no effect, and the statute of limitations was changed to the six-year period prescribed for contracts and promissory notes without seal.

49   See Edwin W. Patterson and George W. Goble, *Cases on Contracts*, pp. 403 ff. (3rd ed. Brooklyn: Foundation Press, 1949), for a discussion of state laws relating to seals. It would seem that a judicious businessman engaged in interstate business would justifiably request a sealed instrument.

CHAPTER V

1   See bill of exchange dated November 4, 1707, reproduced in Appendix C.

2   See bill of exchange dated March 31, 1703, reproduced in Appendix C.

3   Morris, *Select Cases of the Mayor's Court*, pp. 527, 539; see also bill of exchange dated March 25, 1743, reproduced in Appendix C.

4   For ship repairs, *R.N.A.*, VI, pp. 246-47; for traveling expenses, Lloyd Family Papers, p. 35.

5 A sight bill, payable at the time of presentation to the drawee, appears in Morris, *Select Cases of the Mayor's Court*, p. 531 (1704), and Mayor's Court Papers, Box 2 (1699). A bill payable ten days after arrival of a vessel at a given port appears in Mayor's Court Minutes, October 24, 1682, to April 9, 1695, p. 360 (1694), and in Morris, *Select Cases of the Mayor's Court*, p. 539 (1708); for bills at thirty and forty days after sight see "Letters and Papers of Cadwallader Colden," I, p. 51 (1724), and Morris, *Select Cases of the Mayor's Court*, p. 535 (1707).

6 Presentment was made by exhibiting the bill to the drawee and making a demand that he either accept the bill, that is, promise to pay it at the specified time, or pay it immediately. On his refusal, formal protest was made in the presence of a notary public, and a notice was forwarded to the drawer of the bill that it had been dishonored and duly protested. It would seem that oral acceptance was adequate. In one case the issue of acceptance was left to the jury, which held against the alleged acceptor. The defendant who pleaded nonacceptance was Paroculus Parmyter, one of the most unusual lawyers in New York, who held the questionable honor of having been disbarred three times and admitted to practice four times (Mayor's Court Minutes, 1704-1710, pp. 198-99, Harding v. Parmyter [September 4, 1706]; Hamlin, "New York's First Bar Association," p. 364).

7 Allison v. Collings, in Morris, *Select Cases of the Mayor's Court*, p. 531 (1704).

8 *Ibid.*, p. 539 (1708); Papers of James Alexander, Box 10 (1742).

9 During the seventeenth century a twenty-five percent premium applied (*R.N.A.*, VI, pp. 246, 247 [1670]; Mayor's Court Minutes, July 24, 1677, to September 5, 1682, p. 190 [1680]); in the eighteenth century a twenty-percent premium applied (Morris, *Select Cases of the Mayor's Court*, p. 539 [1708]; Papers of James Alexander, 1-7 [1742]).

10 Of the two seventeenth-century cases cited in note 9 the first is by an endorsee, the second by the original purchaser.

11 On a bill of exchange drawn by a party residing in Boston, the New York purchaser authorized a Boston correspondent to institute suit on his behalf; see details related in a case in Mayor's Court to recover on the basis of the Boston judgment for the purchaser (Mayor's Court Minutes, July 24, 1677, to September 5, 1682, p. 190 [1680]).

12 *Ibid.*, p. 252 (1681).

CHAPTER VI

1 Ambrose v. Seaman, Mayor's Court Minutes, December 20, 1763, to January 10, 1764, pp. 134, 143, is an example of a proceeding in bankruptcy by voluntary assignment for the benefit of creditors. Notice was given to creditors by publication in two newspapers. See also *ibid.*, p. 78, where the executrix of an estate confessed judgment provided she be required to pay only a proportion of the total indebtedness (August 9, 1763). Perhaps creditors longed for the older practice of debt imprisonment!

2 *Ibid.*, p. 170, Legett v. Earle (March 24, 1764); for post-Revolutionary con-

tinuance of clause see MS Papers of John McKesson, Bonds, Promissory Notes, New-York Historical Society, Box VII, folder 18 (note of John Padgett).

3 A joint and several note with four signers (Papers of James Alexander, Box 13 [November 13, 1729]). For an example of a creditor asking a master for help to collect a servant's joint and several note see MS Papers of John Tabor Kempe, Miscellaneous Manuscripts, Legal Matters, New-York Historical Society, Box IV (Henry Vawser to William Kempe, January 15, 1755).

4 Mayor's Court Papers, Box 2, Dugdale v. Carr (1775).

5 No specific form seems to have been used. Pleading the statute's effective date see Mayor's Court Minutes, August 7, 1750, to December 7, 1751, p. 16; *ibid.*, 1765 to 1768, pp. 58-63. Cases in which effective date is not pleaded also occur (*ibid.*, 1765 to 1768, p. 161 [1766]).

6 Mayor's Court Papers, Box 2, Obligation Betts to Leydeback.

7 MS Papers of Samuel Jones, Correspondence and Legal Papers, New York Public Library, folder marked 1791-1799.

8 MS Papers of Frederick Ashton DePeyster, New-York Historical Society, Box 4, folder marked Schuyler accounts and receipts 1737-1788. Letters 1 July 1761, 18 August 1761, 4 August 1761, between Peter Schuyler and various individuals.

9 Papers of Samuel Jones.

10 Papers of John Tabor Kempe, Lawsuits A-B, Blouin v. Witmen.

APPENDICES

1 *Doc. Rel. Col. Hist. N.Y.*, III, pp. 306, 403, 420.

2 Notes of George Chalmers, I, p. 22.

3 Edmund B. O'Callaghan, editor, *Documentary History of the State of New York*, I, p. 702. 4 vols. Albany, New York: Weed, Parsons and Company, 1849.

4 *Ibid.*, I, p. 702.

5 Notes of George Chalmers, I, p. 37.

6 O'Callaghan, *Documentary History*, I, p. 703. Of the intervening period little evidence seems to have survived the eighteenth century. In 1711 a report prepared on the port of New York stated that customs revenues amounted to £4,656.1.9 for the period from 1702, but that the revenue should have amounted to £6,274.8.11 (Trade of the Port of New York, fol. 11).

7 Register of Solomon LaChair, p. 336. The entry is dated July 14, 1662. This bill was assigned to LaChair, who endorsed it to another for credit to his account in Holland.

8 Papers of John Wick.

9 *Ibid.*

10 Lloyd Family Papers, p. 157.

11 Papers of James Alexander, Box 1.

12 *Ibid.*

13 *Ibid.*

14 *Ibid.*

15 MS Emmet Collection, New York Public Library.

BIBLIOGRAPHY

MANUSCRIPTS

Abridgment by Roger Mompesson. Columbia University Law Library.

Calendar of the Proceedings of the Court of Assizes, 1665-1672. New York Public Library.

Emmet Collection. New York Public Library.

Extracts on the Court of Assizes 1665-1672. Joseph W. Moulton Manuscript. New-York Historical Society.

John Chambers, Common Place Book (1703-1734). Columbia University Law Library.

Mayor's Court Papers. Benjamin Salzer Collection. Columbia University Special Collections Library.

Minutes of the Mayor's Court, City of New York, November 13, 1674, to September 21, 1675. Office of the New York County Clerk.

Note Book of Joseph Murray. Columbia University Law Library.

Notes of George Chalmers. New York Public Library.

Papers of Abraham DePeyster, 1695-1710. New-York Historical Society.

Papers of Frederick Ashton DePeyster. New-York Historical Society.

Papers of James Alexander. New-York Historical Society.

Papers of John McKesson, Bonds, Promissory Notes. New-York Historical Society.

Papers of John Tabor Kempe, Miscellaneous Manuscripts, Legal Matters. New-York Historical Society.

Papers of John Wick of Northampton, Long Island, New York. Wick-Blachly-Colles Papers. Correspondence and Papers, 1688-1925. New York Public Library.

Papers of Samuel Jones, Correspondence and Legal Papers. New York Public Library.

Register of Solomon LaChair, Notary Public of New Amsterdam 1661-1664, translated by Edmund B. O'Callaghan. Office of the New York City Clerk.

Register of Walewyn van der Veen, Notary Public of New Amsterdam, 1662-1664, translated by Edmund B. O'Callaghan. Office of the New York City Clerk.

Trade of the Port of New York (Colony), 1711 (photostat). New York Public Library.

PUBLISHED SOURCES

A Dialogue Between a Member of Parliament, a Divine, a Lawyer, a Freeholder, a Shopkeeper and a Country Farmer. Anonymous pamphlet published in England in 1703. Columbia University Special Collections Library.

Andrews, Charles M. *The Colonial Period of American History.* 4 vols. New Haven: Yale University Press, 1934-1938.

Beardwood, Alice. *Alien Merchants in England 1350 to 1377, Their Legal and Economic Position.* Cambridge, Massachusetts: Medieval Academy of America, 1931.

Black, Henry Campbell. *Law Dictionary.* Fourth edition. St. Paul, Minnesota: West Publishing Company, 1951.

Bridenbaugh, Carl. *Cities in the Wilderness; the First Century of Urban Life in America, 1625-1742.* New York: Ronald Press, 1938.

Collections of the New-York Historical Society for the Year 1912 (Volume XLV). "Minutes of the Supreme Court of Judicature, April 4, 1693, to April 1, 1701." New York: The Society, 1913.

————— "Proceedings of the General Court of Assizes Held in the City of New York, October 6, 1680, to October 6, 1682." New York: The Society, 1913.

Collections of the New-York Historical Society for the Year 1917 (Volume L). "Letters and Papers of Cadwallader Colden" (Volume I, 1711-1729). New York: The Society, 1918.

Collections of the New-York Historical Society for the Year 1926 (Volume LIX). "Papers of the Lloyd Family of the Manor of Queens Village, Lloyd's Neck, Long Island, New York, 1654-1826" (Volume I, 1654-1752). New York: The Society, 1927.

Collections of the New-York Historical Society for the Year 1934 (Volume LXVIII). "Letters and Papers of Cadwallader Colden, Additional Letters and Papers, 1715-1748" (Volume VIII). New York: The Society, 1937.

Colonial Laws of New York from the Year 1664 to the Revolution. 5 vols. Albany, New York: James B. Lyon, State Printer, 1894.

Dicey, Albert Venn. *Conflict of Laws,* edited by J. H. C. Morris. Sixth edition. London: Stevens and Sons, 1949.

Duffy, John. *Epidemics in Colonial America.* Baton Rouge: Louisiana State University Press, 1953.

Ellis, David M., James A. Frost, Harold C. Syrett, and Harry

J. Carman. *A Short History of New York State.* Ithaca: Cornell University Press, 1957.

Fernow, Berthold, editor. *The Records of New Amsterdam from 1653 to 1674 Anno Domini.* 7 vols. New York: Knickerbocker Press, 1897.

Grotius, Hugo. *The Jurisprudence of Holland,* translated by Robert Warden Lee. 2 vols. Oxford: Clarendon Press, 1926.

Hamlin, Paul M. "New York's First Bar Association." *New York Law Forum,* V (October 1959).

Hamlin, Paul M. and Charles E. Baker, editors. *Supreme Court of Judicature of the Province of New York 1691-1704.* 3 vols. New York: New-York Historical Society, 1959.

Holden, J. Milnes. *The History of Negotiable Instruments in English Law.* London: Athlone Press, 1955.

Holdsworth, William S. *A History of English Law.* Third edition revised. 13 vols. London: Methuen and Company, 1903-1956.

Hough, Charles Merrill. *Reports of Cases in the Vice Admiralty of the Province of New York and in the Court of Admiralty of the State of New York, 1715-1788.* New Haven: Yale University Press, 1925.

Leder, Lawrence H. and Vincent P. Carosso. "Robert Livingston (1654-1728): Businessman of Colonial New York." *Business History Review,* XXX (March 1956).

Morris, Richard B., editor. *Select Cases of the Mayor's Court of New York City 1674-1784.* Washington: American Historical Association, 1935.

Nettles, Curtis P. *The Money Supply of the American Colonies before 1720.* Madison: The University of Wisconsin Press, 1934.

O'Callaghan, Edmund B., editor. *Documentary History of the State of New York.* 4 vols. Albany, New York: Weed, Parsons and Company, 1849-1851.

O'Callaghan, Edmund B., editor. *Documents Relative to the Colonial History of New York.* 15 vols. Albany, New York: Weed, Parsons and Company, 1853-1887.

Paltsits, Victor Hugo, editor. *Minutes of the Executive Council of the Province of New York; Administration of Francis Lovelace, 1668-1673.* 2 vols. Albany: State of New York, 1910.

Patterson, Edwin W. and George W. Goble. *Cases on Contracts.* Third edition. Brooklyn: Foundation Press, 1949.

Rerum Britannicarum Medii Aevi Scriptores, or Chronicles and Memorials of Great Britain and Ireland During the Middle Ages (Volume XII). "Munimenta Gildhallae Londoniensis: Liber Albus, Liber Custumarum, et Liber Horn," edited and translated by Henry Thomas Riley. London: Longmans, Brown, Green, Longmans and Roberts, 1859-1862.

Roberts, William I., III. *The Fur Trade of New England in the Seventeenth Century.* Ann Arbor, Michigan: University Microfilms, 1958.

Sack, Alexander N. *Conflicts of Laws in the History of English Law.* New York: New York University Press, 1937.

Sheppard, William. *A Grand Abridgment of the Common and Statute Law of England.* 2 vols. London: E. Flesher, J. Streater, and H. Twyford, 1675.

Statistical Abstract Supplement: Historical Statistics of the United States, Colonial Times to 1957. Washington: U.S. Department of Commerce, 1960.

Stokes, I. N. Phelps, compiler. *The Iconography of Manhattan Island.* 6 vols. New York: Robert H. Dodd, 1915.

Story, Joseph. *Commentaries on the Conflicts of Laws,* edited by Melville M. Bigelow. Eighth edition. Boston: Little, Brown and Company, 1883.

Whitworth, Sir Charles. *State of the Trade of Great Britain in Its Imports and Exports.* London: G. Robinson, J. Robson, J. Walter, T. Cadell, J. Sewall, 1776.

INDEX

legal system of, 16
population of, 47-48
prosperity in, 9-10, 11
relationship of with British Empire,
    2, 7, 8
trade of, 2, 7-12, 14, 38, 39
Nicolls, Richard, 32
Notaries public, 23, 29-30, 32

O'Callaghan, Edmund B., 47, 49
Ohio River Valley, 43

Palatine Germans, 10
Penal bill, 31, 33, 42
Penal provision in writings obligatory, 2,
    29-30
Pennsylvania, 11
Philadelphia, 9
Piepoudre courts, 17, 25
Piracy, 10
Policies of insurance, 21
Precious metals, 13
Premium on bills of exchange, 40
Privateers, 9-10, 11, 25
Privy Council, 34
Promissory note, 2-3, 21, 35-36, 38, 41,
    42
Promissory Note Act of 1704, 35, 41
Prosperity
    in New Amsterdam, 5-6
    in New York, 9-10, 11

Queen Anne's War, 11, 12

Rensselaerswyck, 23
Reoccupation of New York by the
    Dutch, 7, 26
Restoration, 5
Royal African Company, 10

Sewan, 6-7
Silver, 13
Slave trade, 10
South Seas Company, 2, 12
Southern colonies, 5, 11-12
Spanish embargo, 11
Specialties, 31, 33, 35

State of the Trade of Great Britain,
    45, 47
States General of Holland, 4
Steelyard, 18
Stuyvesant, Peter, 4
Suits on formal writings obligatory, 30-
    31, 32-33, 36
Superior Court of the Dominion of New
    England, 24
Supreme Court of Judicature, 24-25, 35
Sylvester, Margaret, 39

Trade
    along coast of New World, 2, 5, 7, 9,
        12, 39
    Dutch language and standards in, 8
    effects of the English Interregnum
        on, 5
    in fur, 6, 7, 9, 10, 11
    in tobacco, 5-7
    influence of on mercantile law, 2
    of Amsterdam, 5, 7, 8, 9, 12
    of Barbados, 9
    of Boston, 9, 10, 12, 13
    of British Empire, 2, 14
    of England, 5, 6, 9-10, 12, 13, 14, 16-
        18, 34, 45-47
    of London, 9
    of Maryland, 7
    of New Amsterdam, 5-7
    of New England, 5, 7
    of New Netherland, 6, 7
    of New York, 2, 7-12, 14, 38, 39
    of southern colonies, 5, 12
    of Virginia, 5, 7
    of West Indies, 5, 7, 9, 11-12, 13
    with the East, 16-17. *See also* Acts of
        Trade and Navigation
Tryon, William, 43
Tudors, 18

Usury Act of 1660, 33

Venue, 19-20, 27
Vice-admiralty Court of the Province of
    New York, 24-25
Virginia, 5, 7

84

About this book

    The Law Merchant and Negotiable Instruments in Colonial New York 1664 to 1730 was designed by William Nicoll of EDIT, INC. It was set in the composing room of LOYOLA UNIVERSITY PRESS. The text is 12 on 14 Bodoni Book; the reduced matter, 10 on 12; and the notes, 8 on 10. The display type is 12 Bodoni Book caps.

    It was printed by PHOTOPRESS, INC., on WARREN's 60-pound English Finish paper and bound by A. C. ENGDAHL AND COMPANY, INC., in BANCROFT cloth.